EPHESIANS: GOD'S NEW PEOPLE

Malcolm O. Tolbert

CONVENTION PRESS • Nashville, Tennessee

Contents

This book is the text for a course in the subject area Bible Study of the Church Study Course.

Target group: This book is designed for adults and is part of the Church Study Course offerings. The 1963 statement of "The Baptist Faith and Message" is the doctrinal guideline for the writer and editor.

Dewey Decimal Classification Number: 227:5

Printed in the United States of America.

A WORD TO BEGIN ...

For the people of God who yearn to be what God intends and to fulfill their divinely appointed role in the plan of redemption, Ephesians is unsurpassed in importance. The book opens up new vistas of possibilities and judges us to the extent that we fall short. It encourages and inspires us to continue our pilgrimage toward the goal God has for his people.

With these powerful, incisive words, Dr. Malcolm O. Tolbert sets the tone for his thought-provoking book. Dr. Tolbert is the pastor of the First Baptist Church of Gainesville, Georgia. Prior to his present pastorate, he served as a foreign missionary and as professor of New Testament and Greek at the New Orleans Baptist Theological Seminary. Out of this rich background, with keen insight and dedicated skill, Dr. Tolbert shares his understanding of Ephesians.

Dr. Tolbert views the church, under the lordship of Christ, as open evidence of God's tearing down barriers which separate people and of his purpose and ability to create a new people. Christ and his church are keys to God's purpose for unifying his universe.

The January Bible Study for 1980 strongly supports Southern Baptists' Bold Mission enterprise. A new understanding of our mission and purpose as God's new people should inspire us to become involved in the church's ongoing redemptive thrust.

The Ephesians textbook can be used in either personal or group study. In both uses, the Personal Learning Activities at the end of each chapter will help the learner review and fix in mind the material covered. When study is done in a group, the companion Teaching Guide and Study Guide will supply helpful resources for the teacher and member. Guidance for use of the Personal Learning Activities in this textbook will be found in the section headed "The Church Study Course" at the back of the book.

Also at the back of the book is a Church Study Course Credit Request (Form 151). On completion of this book study, the pupil should mail in the completed form to the address indicated. Two copies of the credit award will be mailed to the applicant's church—one for the church's record, the other for the member's own use.

ELI LANDRUM, JR., editor

Acknowledgments

I dedicate this work to my teacher, Dr. Frank Stagg. My personal debt to him cannot be measured. He is the kind of teacher who teaches facts, but more importantly, he helps to change lives. His love for the New Testament and his unflagging dedication to becoming a good interpreter of it have influenced me deeply. Above all, his commitment to Jesus Christ as his personal Lord has inspired me and hundreds of others who have been fortunate enough to sit at his feet.

In preparing this study, I am indebted to Markus Barth. Once in a while, a person has the background, insight, skill, and commitment to produce a truly great commentary. Markus Barth certainly has done this in his two-volume work on Ephesians. Although my indebtedness to his work is documented sparingly in the course of my writing, Markus Barth helped me to form many of my own ideas about the meaning of numerous passages in Ephesians.

Credits

Cover by Dean Shelton; p. 6 Nancy Hayes; p. 17 Phyllis Jolly; p. 21 Yale University Library; p. 25 *Illustrator* photo/David Rogers; p. 31 *Illustrator* photo/David Rogers; p. 38 *Illustrator* photo/David Rogers; p. 44 John Paul Yates; p. 50 *Illustrator* photo/David Rogers/The Louvre; p. 62 *Illustrator* photo/Ken Touchton; p. 64 *Illustrator* photo/Ken Touchton; p. 76 *Illustrator* photo/David Rogers; p. 83 *Illustrator* photo/David Rogers/Ephesus Museum; p. 87 *Illustrator* photo/David Rogers; p. 90 *Illustrator* photo/David Rogers; p. 96 *Illustrator* photo/David Rogers; p. 102 *Illustrator* photo/David Rogers; p. 111 *Illustrator* photo/David Rogers; p. 117 *Illustrator* photo/David Rogers; p. 131 Courtesy of the Royal Ontario Museum, Toronto

The Bible text used in this book is the Revised Standard Version unless otherwise stated.

1

Praise to the God of All Blessing

Ephesians 1:1-14

In our day, one major concern of Christian thinkers and leaders is to discover the nature and purpose of the church in God's plan. Theologians generally agree that the New Testament concept of the church reaches its highest point in Ephesians. The book is the key to understanding the people that God created by the redemptive event of the incarnation. Ephesians occupies a prominent place in biblical studies.

Many scholars consider Ephesians to be the finest expression of Pauline thought. In it, ideas that are germinal in Paul's earlier writings come to full fruition.

For the people of God who yearn to be what God intends and to fulfill their divinely appointed role in the plan of redemption, Ephesians is unsurpassed in importance. The book opens up new vistas of possibilities and judges us to the extent that we fall short. It encourages and inspires us to continue our pilgrimage toward the goal God has for his people.

Some scholars question whether Ephesians is a letter at all. In some ways, it differs from Paul's other letters in that, in it, Paul dealt with great ideas rather than local problems. The book's concern is with the purpose of the church as a whole as that purpose is expressed through a specific congregation. Because of its unusual character, Ephesians has been described as a treatise, a sermon, and a circular letter.

No matter how Ephesians is described, it is cast in the form of a first-

Entrance to Mamertine Prison in Rome, traditional site of Paul's imprisonment. The circular grate covers the hole through which prisoners were lowered to the prison below.

century letter. We have many examples of letter writing from the Hellenistic world that circled the Mediterranean in the first century. The letters commonly begin with (1) the name of the writer, (2) the name of the recipients, (3) a word of greeting, and (4) a prayer of thanksgiving and/or intercession for the recipients. This is the form Paul followed in his letters. Ephesians is no different from his other writings in the structure of its opening.

But Paul differed from other letter writers in the use he made of their conventions. Paul used the conventional form to communicate distinctly Christian ideas. This constituted Paul's creative contribution to letter writing and established the pattern for the early Christian epistle. Paul was the creator; others were imitators.

The Salutation (1:1-2)

In keeping with his own unique style, Paul not only identified himself as the writer of the epistle at the beginning; he also made certain significant statements about himself. In Ephesians 1:1, he called himself "an apostle of Christ Jesus." In the New Testament, the term "apostle" can be a practical synonym of our word *missionary,* one who was sent out by a church to proclaim the gospel. (See Acts 14:4, Rom. 16:7.) It also can mean a commissioned representative of a church. (See 2 Cor. 8:23; Phil. 2:25.)

The word "apostle" also has a restricted sense in the New Testament. Writers used the word to designate those men whom Jesus had chosen and commissioned. In this special sense, Paul called himself an apostle. He had seen the risen Lord and had received his commission to preach the gospel directly from Jesus. (See Rom. 1:1; 1 Cor. 9:1-2; 15:9; 2 Cor. 11:4-5.) In other words, Paul claimed for himself a status equal to that of the original apostles.

How Paul distinguished his religious experience from that of other second generation Christians, we do not know, but he did. When he called himself "an apostle of Christ Jesus," he meant: I am an emissary chosen directly by Jesus Christ to be his personal and special agent in bringing the good news to the Gentiles.

Paul further qualified his apostleship: His role was an expression of the "will of God" (v. 1). What had been effected through Christ Jesus was a faithful execution of God's own decision. God's choice of Paul as an apostle had its place and meaning in the context of God's unfolding plan of redemption, which is the subject of Ephesians.

Paul's conviction that God had called him to his task is a significant key to understanding his thought. He had known hostility and had suffered beatings; even now he was imprisoned. He had experienced ingratitude, opposition, and slander from fellow Christians. From what we can perceive, however, none of this ever caused Paul to be disillusioned to the point that he was ready to turn his back on the church. His voice was stilled only by death.

A person cannot help thinking of the contrast between Paul and many contemporary pastoral ministers. Of course, if a person is mistaken in his call, he shows honesty and courage when he faces up to that fact. But the modern world is filled with people who have given up the pastoral ministry because they have had the kinds of experiences Paul had, although generally not to the same degree. They renounce the pastoral ministry and turn their backs on the church because they are bitter, disillusioned, hurt, or simply because they can make more money in other endeavors. Paul's conviction that God's will was expressed in his Lord's summons would not allow him to abdicate his ministry.

Customarily, Paul added descriptive phrases to the identification of the recipients of his letters. In the first place, in Ephesians he called his intended readers "saints" (v. 1). Our use of the word *saint* places the emphasis on a person's moral character and religious feats. That is not the way Paul used the term. He used the word primarily in keeping with his Old Testament background. In the Old Testament, the word "saint" describes the people who belonged to God (Deut. 7:6).

When Paul called believers saints, he emphasized their relationship to the people of God in the Old Testament. He stressed the gracious, redemptive action of God who had chosen the Hebrews and had made them his people.

Some of the people whom Paul called saints were not morally good. Paul called them saints because he believed they were a part of God's people. The emphasis of the word in this context, therefore, is not on the behavior of believers but on the goodness of the God who had loved them and had redeemed them.

In the King James Version, the readers are identified further as being "at Ephesus" (v. 1). This phrase was omitted by the translators of the Revised Standard Version. This omission points up a textual problem. Some important manuscripts, including the oldest copy of the Pauline epistles, omit the words "in Ephesus."

In addition to the absence of the phrase "in Ephesus" in important manuscripts, Ephesians itself seems to create doubt that Paul wrote the letter to the Ephesian Christians. According to Acts, Paul stayed in Ephesus approximately three years. Therefore, he knew the church and the individuals who composed it in a personal and an intimate way. However, when we read Ephesians we fail to find the kinds of personal and concrete references that we would expect in a letter from Paul to that congregation. Ephesians is the least personal of all Paul's writings. As Markus Barth observed, if Paul wrote to Ephesus, he was addressing a group of Gentiles who had come into the church subsequently to his

ministry there. Many people believe that Ephesians was a circular letter
sent to several churches in western Asia Minor, of which Ephesus was one;
Ephesus may have been the major city to receive the letter, so that this city
became identified strongly with the epistle. This may be the case. We must
admit, however, that we are not sure who the recipients of this letter were.
We do know that they were "saints."

Last of all, Paul addressed himself to people who were "faithful in Christ
Jesus" (v. 1). The word translated "faithful" also may have meant and still
may mean believers. The context alone determines the choice. In this case,
the context is not decisive. The phrase may be used to distinguish Christian saints from Old Testament saints. Both the old community of Israel
and the new community that God was creating could have been called
saints. The difference was the relationship of the new community to the
Christ—Jesus the Messiah. The readers were saints because they were
believers "in Christ Jesus" (v. 1). Most versions, however, translate the
word as "faithful." This rendering emphasizes the believers' way of life
rather than their inward commitment. This approach assumes that the
Christians' faithfulness in words, actions, and relationships was a living
out of their faith.

"In Christ Jesus," a favorite Pauline expression, has various shades of
meaning in different contexts. However, we safely can say that "in Christ
Jesus" emphasizes the believer's relationship to Christ on the one hand
and Christ's centrality in God's redemptive purpose on the other hand.
Whatever the Christian is, whatever he or she does as a believer, whatever
his or her hopes for the future—all are dependent on and are determined
by the person's relationship to Christ Jesus.

The greeting in Ephesians is typically Pauline. He did not use the
common greeting found in contemporary Hellenistic correspondence. In
such correspondence, the common word of greeting was *chairein,* which
literally meant to rejoice. However, Paul made two great words common to
the Christian vocabulary—"grace" and "peace." They served as his greeting to Christian congregations (v. 2).

"Grace" is God's unmerited favor. Redemption is possible only because
God's love reaches out to us when we do not deserve it, when we ignore it,
or when we rebel against it. Paul knew the meaning of grace, for God had
come to him when he was rebelling against God and was totally set against
God's redemptive purpose. Paul had not been seeking, praying, weeping,
or doing anything like these when God had saved him. Rather, Paul had
been on his way to Damascus with murder in his heart. When we try to
interpret grace in Paul's writings, we have to remember that it can be
understood only in the context of his Damascus road experience. He knew
what unmerited favor meant.

"Peace" is a practical synonym for salvation. The term describes the
believer's new existence. Hostility no longer exists between the believer

and God. God is not seen as against the individual but as for the person.
Especially in Ephesians, peace describes the new relationship between the
believer and others. The middle wall has been broken down (Eph. 2:14).
People no longer are classified as Jew or Greek, male or female (Gal. 3:28).
Today, when we largely understand peace in terms of our psychological
orientation, we need to realize that this was not Paul's primary emphasis.
He was not writing about peace of mind or tranquility, although this
certainly may be a consequence of peace. For Paul, peace described the
totally new state into which God's gracious action had helped the believer
to enter. God has brought us to himself and to one another.

God's Plan of Redemption (1:3-14)

Rooted in God's Eternal Choice

Paul opened the main body of Ephesians with a shout of grateful praise.
The shout was not an imperative as most of our Bible translations read.
Paul's words did not summon others to praise God. Rather, that shout was
an outpouring of Paul's heart. His expression was that of a man who had
glimpsed the height, breadth, and depth of God's redemptive activity and
who exulted in his participation in that activity: "Blessed be the God and
Father of our Lord Jesus Christ!" (v. 3).

Who was this God? What was his name? For Paul, as for other early
believers, he was the "Father of our Lord Jesus Christ" (v. 3). The term
"Father" is a metaphor which certainly must not be pressed to make it
coincide with all that the word means in human relationships. To call God
the Father of Jesus stressed the intimate relationship between Jesus and
God. And it affirmed that Jesus' work was to be explained by God's
initiative. Today, whatever the Christian receives in relationship to Jesus
Christ comes from the Father.

Paul knew God, not through the Law or conscience or his study of
Scripture, but through Christ. Today, we begin to know God when we
recognize that he is the Father of Jesus Christ.

Paul praised God for his blessing: God "has blessed us in Christ with
every spiritual blessing in the heavenly places" (v. 3). God's blessing is not
defined clearly here. Paul defined blessing in later verses of this passage.
The blessing is qualified here, however, by five elements of the predicate.

First, the blessing is not a private, personal one. Paul affirmed that God
"has blessed us" (v. 3). When he thought about God's blessing, he did not
think in the way that many of us do. When we say that God has blessed us,
we generally think in personal, private, and even selfish terms. We usually think of good jobs, good health, the love and support of family, and
personal success.

For Paul, God's blessing was the same in wealth or in poverty, in good times or in bad, in personal success or in failure. God's blessing was one that he shared with all believers at all times. This corporate way of thinking and speaking was typically Pauline. He received God's blessing in fellowship with all believers.

God's blessing also is characterized as a "spiritual blessing" (v. 3). "Spiritual" does not mean something vague, sentimental, or otherworldly, divorced from history and human life. All God does is by definition spiritual; God's activity, his gifts, and all that the believer experiences because of his relationship to God is spiritual. All the believer receives and does under the direction of God is spiritual. A spiritual gift is described as coming from God. The idea that God acts in his Spirit also is present in verse 3.

Furthermore, God's blessing is whole, complete. He has blessed us with "every spiritual blessing," or with "all spiritual blessings" (v. 3, KJV[1]). For Paul, however, God's blessing was not to be divided into its various parts. Perhaps we should translate, with Markus Barth, "full spiritual blessing."[2]

God has blessed us "in the heavenly places" or, literally, in the heavenlies (v. 3). The phrase "heavenly places" is not to be understood in terms of geography but in terms of relationship. Wherever God is, is a heavenly place. When we are in relationship with God, we are in a heavenly place. Like the terms peace, saints, and grace, the phrase "heavenly places" is an affirmation of the privileged relationship which the Christian community has with God.

Finally, God's blessing comes to us "in Christ" (v. 3). We receive our blessing from God by virtue of our relationship to Christ. Another way of expressing this truth is to say that God has blessed those who are in the body of Christ—the fellowship of believers. To be in Christ is to be associated with the other members of his body.

In verse 4, Paul began to define in more concrete terms the blessing for which he praised God. One of the major ideas in this whole section is that the blessing is rooted solely in God and has no explanation outside of God's purpose and love.

He chose us "before the foundation of the world" (v. 4). Here, redemption is seen as preeminent over creation. Redemption also is described as independent of history's events and crises. God's purpose of redemption is not the result of a hasty decision. God did not react to an emergency created by sin and rebellion.

God's love is eternal. His purpose of redemption is eternal. What does this truth mean? This concept meant for Paul, and should mean for us, that neither evil, nor fate, nor chance, nor any heavenly or earthly power, nor any experience can separate us from God's love.

The essence of the biblical doctrine of election is God's eternal love. The purpose of that doctrine is to strengthen the believer's confidence in God's ability to save. In spite of evil and suffering, God has everything under control. He is pursuing faithfully his purpose to redeem persons.

The doctrine of election has been distorted in the history of theology by the development of the doctrine of unconditional predestination. According to this doctrine, human choice plays no part in either salvation or damnation; God chooses the saved who cannot resist his grace, and all others are lost.

To say that our salvation is the result of God's purpose which stands outside time and space is to verbalize a thrilling truth. But to say that others are lost because God did not choose to save them makes God a monster. Such a concept rejects the clear teaching of John 3:16 and denies any possibility of human freedom.

God's choice has a purpose that is to be realized in the lives of believers—"that we should be holy and blameless before him" (v. 4). The Christian life includes, as it were, the indicative mood and the imperative mood. We have said that all believers are saints; that is, all are holy by virtue of belonging to God's own people. This concept is the indicative of the Christian faith. Saints, however, live under the imperative of the gospel: They are to be holy and blameless. That is, they are to become what they already are. They are to live up to the special relationship they have received as a gift from God.

For Paul, salvation opened up the possibility for the believer to grow. More than that, salvation guaranteed the achievement of God's purpose. Today, we may falter and fail in our attempts to be what God wants us to be, but we have the confidence that he will complete his work in us. This hope is one of the most important factors in Christian living. However often we fail, we know that God will succeed finally; and so we trust that one day we will become good people, people who love God with all our hearts and who love our neighbors as ourselves.

Paul first defined the goal of election in terms of the character of believers (holy and without blame). In verse 5, he defined the goal in terms of status. God has "destined us in love to be his sons." The word translated "sons" literally means placed as a son, adoption. This image of adoption is found only in Paul's writings. Other writers, such as John, wrote of our relationship to God as our being God's children. By his use of the term meaning adopted as a son, Paul apparently emphasized the fact that what we are depends totally on God. We are not children by natural birth or by merit. We owe our status before God to the free choice of his grace.

Adoption is emphasized further by the concluding phrase in verse 5, "according to the purpose of his will." "Purpose" literally means "good pleasure" (KJV) and is a practical synonym of will. The former differs from the latter in its emotional connotation. Our redemption is according to the purpose of God, and our redemption is something in which God delights.

I agree with the Revised Standard Version which puts "in love" with verse 5 rather than verse 4, although the Greek text is ambiguous about this. (See the KJV, for example.) God's eternal purpose is explained by his love. His love is the reason why his purpose is dependable. In many discussions of election, this all-important, central aspect of love is left out. The love of God is *agape,* which is not dependent on human merit or response. *Agape* is constant, never-diminishing, never-changing love! *Agape* emanates from God and is the central expression of his character. His redemptive purpose has its source in love and is executed in love. We can depend on God to carry his purpose through to the end because of his unfailing love.

God is the sovereign God whose election determines our salvation. But some people have made him into a grim, forbidding personage; they have interpreted his actions as arbitrary, inscrutable, and harsh. This concept of God misses altogether the central theme of Paul's doctrine of election. God's election is not harsh, arbitrary, and inscrutable; it is determined solely by love.

The realization that God chooses to redeem us in love will lead to "the praise of his glorious grace" (v. 6). Certainly, Paul praised God's grace as he composed this great hymn. God's grace also is praised every time a group of believers assembles to worship God, their redeemer.

The last part of verse 6 is difficult to translate in a way that emphasizes grace as the Greek text does. The verb *echaritosen* is a cognate of the noun *charis,* grace. We might translate *echaritosen* literally: with which he has begraced us in the Beloved. "Beloved" is a messianic title. Any group or individual who is chosen by God to participate in his redemptive purpose may be called God's beloved. Although the word *beloved* may be applied to anyone—for example, a fellow believer—it belongs to Jesus in a special sense. "Beloved" is the title given to the One whom God chose to be the means through which his grace flows to believers.

Realized Through Jesus Christ
In verse 7, Paul shifted from the eternal to the historical. In the preceding passage, the emphasis had been God's eternal choice, in love, as the source of our redemption. Paul then turned his attention from the eternal to the event in history in which God's eternal purpose was actualized. That event was the cross. "Through his blood" (v. 7)—that is, through the sacrificial death of Jesus—redemption becomes a reality for the believer.

"Redemption" (v. 7) is a typical Pauline metaphor. From Paul's viewpoint, people's basic problem was their helpless enslavement to the mighty power of sin, or the flesh. People need liberation. If they are to be free, a power greater than the power of sin must free them. Paul believed that God had emancipated believers by the cross and had moved them into the sphere of his own love and power.

"The forgiveness of our trespasses" (v. 7) is not a typical Pauline phrase. The words emphasize human guilt and responsibility for our predicament. We are rebels against God, willful violators of his will. We need forgiveness. In Christ, God does forgive us.

Forgiveness and redemption throw light on two important facets of our salvation. God does forgive us; at the same time, he frees us from sin's dominion. We come under his rule, which is more powerful than sin's rule.

The forgiveness of trespasses is modified by the phrase "according to the riches of his grace which he lavished upon us" (vv. 7-8). Our redemption is no mean, meager thing. Salvation is not according to our merit, tears, sorrow, or any other human achievement or action. Redemption is according to grace, lavish grace. Our redemption is as great, as lasting, as wide, as universal in scope, as invincible as God's grace.

In the preceding verses, Paul praised God for God's redemption that (1) has its roots in his eternal purpose, (2) is characterized by his lavish grace, (3) has brought the believer into a new relationship with him and other people, and (4) has given the believer a new future. Only when he reached verses 9 and 10 did Paul indicate the scope of God's eternal purpose, in which the redemption of persons constitutes such a central part.

The exact relation of "wisdom and insight" to the rest of verse 9 is not clear. Are "wisdom and insight" God's gifts to the believer, who is thereby able to perceive what God is doing? Or, are they descriptive of the way God relates to the believer in revealing himself? God's actions are not arbitrary, random, or senseless. "Grace" is free and overflowing, but it is not given thoughtlessly.

To choose between the two options is difficult. Both are true. God acts in a wise way, and he has endowed us with the capacity to perceive what he is doing.

God is not only a loving and saving God; he is also a God who reveals himself to his children, making known to them the secret of his purpose. He has made known to us "the mystery of his will" (v. 9). "Mystery" is a literal, but not the best, translation of the word. "Secret" is a better translation. God's purpose had been secret. True, the prophets had received glimpses of his secret. But they did not know what God really was doing. (See Col. 1:26.) No one had grasped his plan in its totality. No one had seen God's purpose in its greatness and grandeur. In Jesus Christ, however, the secret had been revealed. In the light of Jesus' death and resurrection, and with the Holy Spirit's insight, Paul and other Christians could fit the pieces of the puzzle together in order to see the whole picture.

The word "mystery" was used to describe the central aspect of the so-called mystery religions of the Greco-Roman world. In them, however, the secrets of life, the world, and salvation were available only to the initiated. These secrets were revealed to the initiated in ways that kept the secrets hidden from the less enlightened of mankind. The initiates were bound not to reveal to others their rites of induction into the mystery religions. To do so was considered blasphemy.

But Jesus' Father had not reserved his secret for an elite group. Indeed, from Paul's perspective, the opposite was true. God's secret is for everybody—rich and poor, Jew and Gentile, free and slave.

God's word is to be shouted from the housetops to everyone; it is not revealed in the inner sanctum of a temple to a special clique. God's word is to be proclaimed in the marketplace, in the synagogue, in people's assemblies.

If people do not know God's secret, the reason is their stubborn refusal to receive it. People often say, "I do not hear God speaking." To tell them about Christ and his incarnation and to ask them, Are you really listening? is appropriate.

The scope of God's open secret is elucidated in verse 10. Much debate and uncertainty exist about the exact meaning of some of the words in the verse. Nevertheless, the major message is clear. God's purpose goes beyond the redemption of individuals. His purpose even goes beyond the creation of his new people, the church, as important as that is. He intends to put all the divided, fragmented universe together again! His purpose is to bring harmony out of the discord produced by the evil and rebellion of the universe.

For Paul, the problem of evil and rebellion against God transcended its human and worldly manifestations. A rift exists in the universe. Paul believed that the hostility among human beings was only one expression of a rebellion of cosmic proportions against God. "The power of the air" (Eph. 2:2) also was arrayed against God. But God was at work, dealing with the problem of rebellion in all its dimensions.

Paul indicated that God's revealed secret had to do with "a plan for the fulness of time" (v. 10). Let us look at some of the particulars of verse 10. "Plan" translates the Greek word *oikonomian,* from *oikonomia,* from which our word *economy* is derived. The word has two primary meanings, either of which is a possible interpretation of the term's significance in this context. The word can refer to a plan or arrangement by which something—for example, a household or a kingdom—is managed. Plan or arrangement is the meaning which the Revised Standard Version's translators gave the word in this context. Most of the translations adopt this interpretation. What God has revealed is his eternal plan that now is being executed in Jesus Christ.

Oikonomia also may refer to the office of the administrator—to his role as administrator. The word is understood in this way by Barth, who translated the phrase in question: "that he should administer the days of fulfillment.[3] In other words, Christ is the administrator of God's redemptive purpose. This is a possibility, but the first option seems to be preferable.

The "fulness of time" (v. 10) means the moment God chose to set his plan of redemption in motion. Everything that God had done before was preparatory, leading to the moment when everything was just right for his purpose.

Why did God decide that the times were full, that this was the right moment? For centuries preachers have pointed to the first-century-world's heart hunger that made people eager for the gospel. They also have talked about the Hellenistic world that was united politically and culturally, thus making the missionary task easier. That Paul had anything like this in mind, however, is doubtful.

God's calendar is not determined by human considerations. He alone decides his calendar. Since God had acted in Jesus Christ to execute his plan, Paul believed that this action had taken place at the right moment no matter what the conditions were from the human point of view.

The verb translated "to unite" (v. 10) in the Revised Standard Version is susceptible to various meanings, as may be seen from the different translations. Two of the better-known variations are "to sum up all things" (ASV[4]) and to "gather together" (KJV). People who can work with the Greek text see something that is not evident in the English translations. The word for head is a component of the compound Greek verb that the Revised Standard Version translates "to unite." This may be the reason that Paul used the relatively infrequent word at this point. Christ is the head in whom or under whom God's purpose to bring about unity is being consummated.

God's unity is to comprehend "all things" (v. 10). To make sure that the cosmic scope of God's plan was understood, Paul added: "things in heaven and things on earth." Paul understood that disunity was a major expression of evil. He believed, however, that the alienation so characteristic of the universe had a limited scope. God was working to put his universe back together through Christ.

The Church, Evidence of God's Purpose

We may ask: How do we know that God is engaged in putting a broken universe together again? Where can we see concrete evidence of God's redemptive, reconciling activity? Is Paul's idea anything more than wishful thinking?

For Paul, the answer to such questions was the church. In God's new people, we see the unmistakable proof that God is on his way to realizing his goal. The church is the group of people in which unity has prevailed over the forces of hate and prejudice. Bringing together erstwhile hostile Jews and Gentiles was the clue to God's cosmic purpose. God already has done something. This incredible work of reconciliation is the theme of

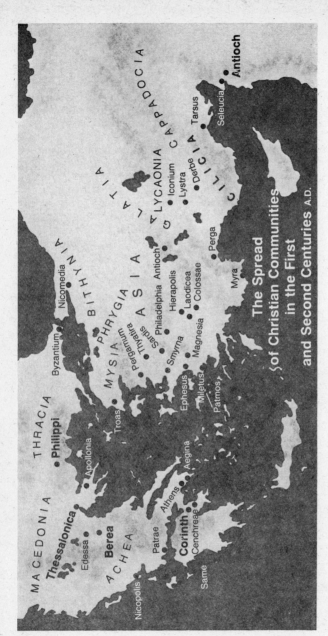

Map showing geographical context of Ephesus

verses 11-14.

Christ is the person in whom God's uniting power is at work. This working through Christ is according to God's own purpose, as Paul wrote in verse 11. Paul further emphasized that God pursued his purpose independent of any pressure or plan outside himself. God does what he does according to the counsel of his will, and his independence alone is the clue to his activity.

Believing Jews had found their place in God's redemptive activity in Christ. When Paul contrasted "we" and "you," as he did in verses 12-13, he was speaking of Jews and Gentiles. "We" referred to the Jews, among whom Paul also found his place. "You" designated the Gentiles.

That Paul wrote first about the Jews is clear from the description found in verse 12. The people he described were those "who first hoped in Christ (the Messiah)." Paul was well aware of the central role played by the Jews in God's redemptive activity. They had received the promises concerning the Messiah. They had hoped for his coming long before the Gentiles had heard about him.

Believing Jews recognized that Jesus was the fulfillment of their hopes. Their lives no longer were characterized by waiting and hoping for the coming Deliverer, but by the "praise of his glory" (v. 12). Praise that arises out of gratitude is the keynote of a redeemed people.

Believing Jews were in Christ, and the same was true of believing Gentiles. The distance between Jews and Gentiles had been overcome. They were in the same sphere in Christ.

The process for the Gentiles was not that of moving from hope in the Messiah to belief in Jesus as its fulfillment. Rather, their salvation was the indirect result of mission by believers. Of course, Christ had saved them, but he had used believers to convey the good news. The Gentiles heard the true word—the gospel. They believed, and they were included in God's people (v. 13).

That Paul connected the sealing with the Holy Spirit to his remarks about Gentiles is interesting. Of course, all believers, whether Jew or Gentile, received the Spirit when they accepted Christ. But the fact that Gentiles were sealed with the Spirit had a special significance for Paul.

The Holy Spirit has two functions in the believing community. The first is described by the verb translated "were sealed" (v. 13). The seal was used in the ancient world as a guarantee of authenticity, as a mark of ownership. When a king wrote a document, he sealed it with wax and impressed on the wax the image of his seal. This sealing was evidence that the document was authentic, that it really came from him.

The Holy Spirit's presence in believers' lives marked them as God's property. The Spirit's presence authenticated their claim to belong to God because it was a testimony that God had accepted them. In Acts 10:44-48, during Peter's sermon, the manifestation of the Holy Spirit in the Gentile hearers overcame Jewish reluctance to baptize them.

That the Gentiles had been sealed with the Spirit was especially important to Paul. Their sealing was the irrefutable evidence that the Gentiles
really belonged to God.

Paul declared that the Spirit "is the guarantee of our inheritance" (v.
14). The King James Version has "the earnest of our inheritance." The
guarantee or the earnest was the first payment made by a person as a
pledge that he would carry through on a business deal.

Paul did not believe that Christians receive in this age all that God will
give them. God has promised us an inheritance that we shall receive in the
future. In the meantime, "until we acquire possession of it" (v. 14), God has
given us the Spirit as a pledge that he will fulfill his promise.

We know that we belong to God because he has given us his Spirit. We
are confident that what we enjoy now in the new community of the Spirit is
but the first installment on our glorious, future inheritance.

Meaning for Life

One of modern people's real problems in affluent, industrial western
society is the feeling of insignificance. So many people are engaged in
work that is boring and meaningless. They do not sense the lift that comes
from feeling that what they are doing is worthwhile. They feel that they
really do not matter in any important way.

The opposite was true with Paul. He was a tentmaker by trade, but his
joy and meaning in life did not come from making tents. I am sure he
experienced some satisfaction in the ability to provide for his needs. Also, I
am sure he was grateful that his skills made it possible for him to pursue
his ministry in a place like Corinth.

Paul's real thrill and challenge in living came from the possibility of
participating in God's plan of redemption. This was something that was
genuinely worthwhile. In comparison with God's great enterprise, all
other endeavors were secondary, insignificant, and limited.

The believer never will feel that life is dull, drab, and meaningless if he
or she gains the perspective that can be perceived in Ephesians. The
Christian has a part in the greatest ongoing venture in the world. God's
person is involved in what God is doing. The associates of God's child are
all of God's children around the world. The believer's destiny is to rejoice
with God and God's people when the thrilling adventure of his or her life
reaches its assured fruition.

When our vision becomes as wide as Paul's, we shall experience the
same thrill and joy he experienced as we identify with what God is doing in
our day.

1. From the King James Version. Subsequent quotations are marked KJV.

2. Markus Barth, *The Anchor Bible: Ephesians,* 2 vols. (Garden City, New York: Doubleday & Company, 1974), 1:76.

3. Ibid. 1:76.

4. From the *American Standard Version* (London: Thomas Nelson & Sons, 1901). Subsequent quotations are marked ASV.

Personal Learning Activities

1. Because of its unusual character, the book of Ephesians has been described as (choose the correct responses from the following list):
   _____(1) A gospel
   _____(2) A treatise
   _____(3) A sermon
   _____(4) A circular letter
2. Ephesians is cast in the form of a first-century_____
   (Choose the proper response from the list.)
   (1) History
   (2) Biography
   (3) Letter
   (4) Novel
3. Letters in the Hellenistic world of the first century commonly began with (choose the correct answers from the following list):
   _____(1) The date
   _____(2) The name of the writer
   _____(3) The name of the recipient(s)
   _____(4) A word of greeting
   _____(5) The address of the writer
   _____(6) A prayer for the recipients
4. Paul identified himself as the writer of Ephesians. True_____
   False_____
5. Match the two lists, linking term with definition:

   _____(1) Apostles
   _____(2) Saints
   _____(3) Grace
   _____(4) Peace
   _____(5) Heavenly places
   _____(6) *Agape*

   (a) Constant, never-diminishing love
   (b) The unmerited favor of God
   (c) Men chosen and commissioned by Jesus
   (d) Wherever God is
   (e) The totally new state of the believer
   (f) The people of God

6. Paul used the word mystery to mean (select the correct response from the list):
   ____(1) Something beyond understanding
   ____(2) His own personal secret
   ____(3) God's secret made known
7. To Paul, the ____ was the evidence of God's purpose to bring unity to the universe. (Choose the proper answer from the following list.)
   (1) Bible
   (2) Church
   (3) Law
   (4) Resurrection

Answers: 1. (2), (3), (4); 2. (3); 3. (2), (4), (6); 4. *True*; 5. (1) *c*, (2) *f*, (3) *b*, (4) *e*, (5) *d*, (6) *a*; 6. (3); 7. (2).

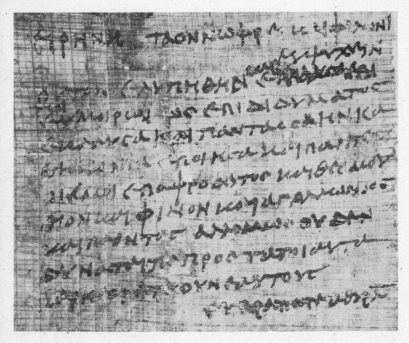

Letter from an Egyptian lady to a friend who had lost a son. The letter is dated in the first century A.D.

2

Paul's Prayer for His Readers

Ephesians 1:15-23

Gratitude for Faith and Love (1:15-16)

In Ephesians 1:1-14, Paul wrote about what God had done for the church. Then he wrote about his own relationship to his readers. The Revised Standard Version does not emphasize Paul's reference to himself in the statement found in verses 15-16 as much as the Greek does. In the Greek text, the subject is "I also" and not just "I" (v. 15). Paul used the same kind of emphatic reference to himself in 3:1,13; 4:1.

Paul knew that his role as the apostle to the Gentiles was important. He expressed his high sense of calling in emphatic personal references found in his letters. Because his role was important, what he did and said should have carried weight with the churches.

Ephesians 1:15-23 is a prayer. First, Paul gave the reason for his prayer. He had heard of his readers' faith and love.

We should note two points here. In the first place, this is one of the possible indications that Paul did not know at least some of his readers personally. If he had been writing to the Ephesians with whom he had spent three years, he would have known about the quality of their life as a church from personal experience, and not from hearsay.

Next, the word *love* is missing from some important manuscripts. Some versions reflect this text in their translations. The truth is that the basic meaning of the reference is not changed. Paul believed that a faithful relationship to Jesus Christ and toward the saints always expressed itself in terms of love.

Most versions contain references to both "faith" and "love." This probably is correct. Paul's expression of thanksgiving showed what was important to him in the life of the church. We are made aware of the contrast between his way of thinking and ours. When we speak of great churches, we generally have in mind the buildings they build, the money they raise, and the numbers on their rolls. These ways of measuring greatness were totally foreign to Paul. Of supreme importance to Paul was the faith and love that the churches expressed. These attributes are difficult to measure. To put them in statistical tables is impossible, for they depend on the activity of God, not of people.

Influenced as we are by the values of the world, we tend to measure greatness in other ways. We can get multitudes together, build huge buildings, and raise large sums of money without any reference to God. The world scores huge successes all the time. If pastors took Paul's approach, however, they no longer could compare their own efforts with those of fellow ministers to the discredit of their fellows. Being weak, insecure, and sinful, we probably shall continue to measure our success in the world's terms.

Paul wrote: "I have heard of your faith in the Lord Jesus" (v. 15). But faith is inward and unseen. One cannot know of a person's faith until it becomes outward, expressed in courage when encountering difficulties, in responsible Christian living, in changed attitudes and relationships, and in confidence when facing death. Perhaps, therefore, we should translate the word as faithfulness. Faith in Jesus is manifested openly, concretely.

Another thought underlies Paul's expression. Faith is not valid in and of itself. In fact, if what we call faith does not have the proper object, it is credulity or superstition. In the Greek text, "faith in the Lord Jesus" (v. 15) is a closely knit phrase. Faith has no point of validity unless it is directed toward Jesus. Anything else that we call faith in a religious sense lacks validity and substance.

A great deal that is unknown lies behind the statement: "I have heard of your faith in the Lord Jesus" (v. 15). Precisely what had Paul heard that had convinced him of the genuineness of his readers' faith? Times of trial and persecution may have arisen. The churches may have been under tremendous pressures to deny their Lord. If so, they had come through those trials victoriously.

The coin has another side. One aspect of the believer's faithfulness toward Jesus Christ is his relationship to other believers. Paul also had heard of the love his readers had expressed "toward all the saints" (v. 15). Once again, love may be thought of as inward and, thus, not susceptible to human discernment. Love in the New Testament, however, is primarily a way of relating and acting. Love is doing rather than feeling. More than this, love is a way of relating that does not depend on the actions, status, or personality of the person loved.

Paul had heard of his readers' love because it had been expressed in concrete, compassionate deeds. The readers' love had been directed "toward *all* the saints" (v. 15). This love was a Godlike love because it had transcended the barriers of culture, race, and nation. Christian love is based on the recognition that all believers are God's children. If all believers are God's children, then they are all brothers and sisters—members of the same family.

Other credentials a church may have do not matter if the important elements of faith and love are missing. A church is not measured by God on the basis of its bustle and activity, its size and wealth, or its orthodoxy.

What good results from our subscribing to a list of doctrines considered to be fundamental if we do not have and express God's love? To say that we believe in Jesus' virgin birth, atoning death, or glorious resurrection is no substitute for our failure to accept the people whom God has accepted. Orthodoxy does not atone for our failure to recognize God's children as our brothers and sisters.

If Ephesians has a fundamental doctrine, that doctrine is: A saving relationship with Jesus Christ means being incorporated into his body. The reason why prejudice is one of the most basic sins is that it denies what God is doing. Prejudice obstructs God's ultimate purpose, which is to bring together all believers in one family.

When Paul wrote that his readers loved all the saints, he had in view the process of God's forming a family of believers. In these believers, the ancient cleavage between Jew and Gentile had been overcome. God's purpose of redemption was at work in them. They were truly the body of Christ.

Paul recognized the presence of faith and love to be a miracle of grace. He did not brag on the believers for having faith and love; rather, he thanked God for what God and God alone had brought about. Believers are what they are because of God's powerful presence and action in their midst.

Prayer for Spiritual Insight (1:17-18)

In verses 17-18, Paul moved from thanksgiving to intercession. The sensitive Christian always is grateful to God for what God already has done among his people. Gratitude is one of the Christian life's great graces.

Many people focus so much on inadequacies and failures that they do not

Double Church of Mary at Ephesus. The first building dates to the
Roman period and was converted into a church.

have room for gratitude. Some people, including pastors, always emphasize negative elements or factors in the life of the church. Paul had the
habit of emphasizing the positive, especially at the beginning of his letters, and of thanking God for the good things.

We always are aware that God has not yet finished his work in his
church. He has more to do, more to give, more to reveal. That gratitude
should be followed by intercession, therefore, is appropriate.

Intercession, and not harsh criticism, is the proper role of the great
Christian leader. As Dietrich Bonhoeffer, one of the most thoughtful
Christians of recent times, has remarked, we should not be our brother's
accusers before God. Nor should we become critics or gossips before people.
To gossip about those for whom we sincerely have prayed probably is not
possible.

First of all, in verses 17-18, Paul pointed out that God is the source of the
gifts that the churches need. God is a generic name; the word can be used
for gods of any and all kinds. But God is identified specifically for the
Christian. He is the "God of our Lord Jesus Christ" (v. 17).

The use of the phrase "God of our Lord Jesus Christ" was, to be sure, an
unusual way for New Testament writers to identify God. A more typical
phrase would identify God as the Father of Jesus Christ. An early group of
people whom we call Arians seized on this verse as their proof text for
arguing against the divinity of Jesus. This misuse of the verse shows the
error in the proof text method, especially when the method is used to
justify so basic a doctrine. A singular and unusual passage never should be
employed as the foundation of a central belief. Other passages make clear
that Paul believed in the divinity of Jesus. (See Phil. 2:6.)

What did Paul mean when he wrote about the God of Jesus Christ? For
Paul, God was above all the God who comes to people in Jesus Christ. He
was the God whom Jesus revealed and served. This was the God about
whom Jesus talked and to whom he prayed. He was the God who made
Jesus the sphere of his gracious, redeeming activity. Paul directed his
prayer toward the God to whom his Lord also had prayed.

Furthermore, God is the "Father of glory" (v. 17). "Father" underlines
God's relationship to believers as the one who loves them, cares for them,
and meets their needs. "Glory" describes God's loftiness and majesty; he is
a Father, but he is a transcendent Father. Because of who he is, God's
possibilities for answering Paul's prayer were limitless.

Paul stressed the believers' need for the capacity to perceive what God
wanted to show them. He asked that God give them a "spirit of wisdom and
of revelation" (v. 17). Whether the reference is to the Holy Spirit or to the
new spirit given to the believer is not clear in the text. Probably the latter
was Paul's thought here. The emphasis, however, is on the result of the
Holy Spirit's activity in the believer's life. The capacity to understand the
things of God was and is a product of the presence and activity of God's

Spirit in the Christian's life.

This new spirit created by God's Spirit is characterized by "wisdom" and "revelation." "Wisdom" is the capacity to think, to make decisions, and to act in accordance with God's purposes. The wise person is not the one who knows a lot of facts but the one who walks in the Lord's ways.

The "spirit of revelation" is the capacity to receive new words from God. As we receive each new word from God, this, in turn, will determine the way we live. That is, as revelation is incorporated and determines our decisions and actions, it becomes wisdom.

Paul believed that the unregenerate person had no possibility of understanding the words and acts of God. The unbeliever does not possess the capacity to receive the insights that God gives. The Spirit gives us eyes to see and ears to hear.

The goal of this wisdom and revelation is "the knowledge of him" (v. 17). In our text, a better translation of the Greek word rendered "knowledge" might be full or genuine knowledge. The goal of the Christian life is to know God fully. This knowledge, we must stress, is not simply factual knowledge. Such knowledge is not just knowing about God; it is knowing God himself. We know God in our relationship with him. This is true because God is not just a fact or a concept or a power. Above all, he is a personal God who is known in faith and love as we interact with him in life's situations.

As Paul wrote in another letter, our knowledge at the present is partial (1 Cor. 13:9). A time will come, however, when we shall know as we are known (1 Cor. 13:12). Paul believed that God leads the Christian in this life toward that heavenly goal, which should be the central desire of the believer's life.

Paul added: "having the eyes of your hearts enlightened" (v. 18a). This phrase is parallel to the preceding one. A person to whom God has given a spirit of wisdom and revelation has an enlightened heart. In biblical thought, the heart was the center of intellect and will. Paul prayed that God's Spirit would act on the minds of believers so that they would be able to perceive what God wanted to reveal to them.

People whose minds are not enlightened by God's Spirit can know only the things of this world. But Paul believed that God gives his people the capacity to see beyond the present and immediate. They can, at least in part, perceive the future to which God is leading them. This future is expressed as "the hope to which he has called you" (v. 18b). The calling here is that initial calling by which individuals are incorporated into God's people. God's call is more than a summons or an invitation. It describes God's activity in reaching out to us, making us aware of himself, drawing us to him, and making us a part of his people. The calling is the beginning of the believer's existence. The hope is involved in it and is its fulfillment.

Paul described hope further as the "riches of his [God's] glorious inheritance in the saints" (v. 18b). The phrase as it stands in the Greek text and the English translation is ambiguous. The words can refer to what God himself will inherit. God does inherit something through his work of redemption. He inherits the saints—that is, the people who belong to him. This is a possible interpretation of Paul's phrase. However, it is the least likely one.

More likely, Paul's phrase refers to the inheritance that God reserves for us, his people. This inheritance is a glorious one, and the word "glorious" points to the fact that God will distribute the inheritance among his people in the hereafter. In 1:18b Paul struggled against language limitations, for he could not perceive and describe exactly what the believer will receive in the future; he could point only to the inheritance's character. The Christian's inheritance is indescribably rich; it is to be received in glory and shared with all the saints.

Prayer for Knowledge of God's Power (1:19-21)

Is the Christian's hope only a vague, sentimental wish? Is it just a baseless projection of a believer's thoughts erected as a defense against the despair of the human situation? No! The God who makes promises also has the power to fulfill them.

Once again, Paul knew that he was attempting to express the inexpressible as he heaped synonym on top of synonym for power. His style is awkward, but the effect is impressive. He knew that if the believer is to live in faith and hope amidst the struggles of this life, he or she must be confident that God is able to fulfill his promises. Therefore, Paul prayed that his readers might know "the immeasurable greatness of his power" in believers (v. 19).

In the Greek text of verse 19, Paul pressed into service four different words for power. The English versions struggle to translate these in a meaningful way. The various shades of meaning possessed by the four words probably are not important in this context. Paul simply tried to say that God's power is great beyond measure.

Power of the Resurrection

God demonstrated the greatness of his power on behalf of believers in the Christian gospel's central event—Christ's resurrection. Paul separated the various stages in this event and showed that each stage is meaningful and applicable to the believer's life. (See Ephesians 2.)

First, God's power was manifested in his deed "when he raised [Christ] from the dead" (1:20a). For Paul, Jesus Christ's resurrection was the most crucial part of the gospel. All else depended on it. As far as Paul was concerned, the truth, effectiveness, and relevance of the gospel were determined by Christ's resurrection. Paul's gospel was the gospel of a risen Lord.

Paul was a Christian because he had met Jesus Christ after Christ's crucifixion and knew from that encounter that Christ was not dead but alive. This was the truth among all truths that really mattered, and all of Paul's understanding of the Old Testament had to be changed in the light of this incredible event. The basis of his theology was the resurrection.

Christians today generally have not taken Jesus' resurrection with the same seriousness as Paul. By and large, we have failed to sense what was so clear to Paul: If Christ is risen, Christian faith is validated; and if Christ is not risen, Christian faith is a colossal mistake.

A college student heard some of her ideas about Jesus attacked in a religion class. She was shaken badly, for her ideas about Jesus were precious to her. But Paul would not have been shaken by the diatribe, for the attacker(s) did not attempt to challenge the resurrection of Christ. From Paul's point of view, if the resurrection fails, all is lost; if it stands (and he believed it does), all is well. Any ideas about Jesus, other than the resurrection, are subsidiary; they may be appraised calmly and brought into line with the great central truth, but they are not primary for faith. The Christian gospel stands or falls on the fact of Jesus' death and resurrection and on nothing else.

Power Which Enthroned Christ

Paul believed that by God's power, Jesus had been raised from the dead. He knew this because of his personal encounter with the risen Lord on the Damascus road. But he also believed something else. He believed that God's power had elevated Jesus to a position of supreme and unchallenged lordship. God gave Jesus a position "at his right hand in the heavenly places" (v. 20). Today, we recognize, of course, that such descriptions are metaphorical. The position at the right hand was reserved by a ruler for the most trusted and powerful person in his realm. Paul used that figure to assert that Christ occupied the place of highest honor and authority. Christ's authority was secure from any rival.

Christ had been enthroned "far above all rule and authority and power and dominion" (v. 21). The names Paul listed were titles given in various religious circles to angelic or spiritual powers. Paul made the list comprehensive by adding the phrase "and above every name that is named" (v. 21). In other words, none of the powers that people believed in was excluded, whether real or imaginary. These spiritual powers could be either good or bad. From the context, we would conclude that Paul thought

of the hostile powers—those that rebelled against God and held sinners in
their sway.

Paul believed in spiritual powers, both good and evil. He believed that
spiritual or angelic powers were in the service of God; some were in
rebellion against God. What distinguished Paul from many others was his
lack of speculative opinions about the spiritual powers. He knew that his
life in Christ was secured against any enemy, even those that were
associated with the "power of the air" (Eph. 2:2).

Many first-century people believed that their lives were under the
power of spiritual forces. Often they associated those spiritual forces with
the stars. Also, their belief in fate was strong. People felt that they were
helpless to do anything about their destiny; therefore, to struggle against
these spiritual powers was useless.

People's strong sense of fate was one reason why the gospel was such
good news. God's power was greater than all other powers. The Lord of the
church was sovereign over all controlling powers. No power could threaten
those who were under Christ's lordship. This glorious truth is affirmed in
Romans 8:38-39 and elsewhere. Even though our vocabulary has changed
from that of the first century, the truth remains vibrant and contemporary. Life never is hopeless, for we are not victims of change or fate. Our
lives are under the supreme lordship of a God who loves us and whose
purpose for us cannot be thwarted.

The sovereignty of Christ was established "not only in this age but also
in that which is to come" (v. 21). The present age is the one in which evil
still is active. The coming age will be marked by the complete overthrow of
the evil powers. In spite of evil's apparent power in this age, Christ already
is Lord. Furthermore, Christ's exaltation by the power of God is not
temporary; it is eternal. This was Paul's deep conviction.

Christ, the Head of the Church (1:22-23)

Paul expressed Christ's eternal exaltation from another point of view. By
God's power, all other powers were made subject to Christ. They have been
subjugated and put "under his feet" (v. 22). This is the image of the
successful conqueror. Christ's victory is complete. The enemies of God and
of believers have been subjugated completely. They lie vanquished at the
feet of the church's conquering and sovereign Lord.

Paul climaxed his description of God's power as being operative in Jesus
Christ who was raised from the dead, was elevated to a place of transcendent authority, was made sovereign over all spiritual powers, and was
given to the church to be its head.

Of course, God gave Christ to the church to be its head. For Paul, this

Marble slab over the place where tradition says Jesus' body was laid. The slab is in the traditional tomb of Jesus in Jerusalem. The empty tomb is evidence of God's resurrection power.

was an expression of God's incredible grace. Now the picture was complete: Christ died *for the church*. He was raised from the dead and elevated above all other powers *for the church*. He was given to the church to be its head. The secret of the church's victory was not and is not in some human being or in any group of people. The secret is not in sophisticated programs or in the church's numerical size. The secret of the church's triumph is in its head, who is the sovereign Lord of the universe.

Verse 22*b* is ambiguous in the Greek text. This ambiguity is reflected in the various translations. The Revised Standard Version translates: God "has made him the head over all things for the church." *The Jerusalem Bible* renders: God "made him, as the ruler of everything, the head of the Church."[1] *The New English Bible* reads: God "appointed him as supreme head to the church."[2]

The question is: Did Paul mean that Christ was the "supreme head to the church," as in *The New English Bible?* Or, was he stressing Christ's rule over the universe as well as over the church? The latter probably is correct, for the church's Lord is none other than the One who rules the universe.

The entire book of Ephesians is about the church. For the first time in the epistle, however, we encounter the word *ekklesia*. In the New Testament, the word *ekklesia* most often is used to designate the church. Probably, the word is best understood as the New Testament equivalent of the Old Testament *qahal*. This Hebrew word designates the people of God. This is its primary meaning. This people's special character comes about because they belong to God.

The New Testament follows the lead of the Old Testament. Sometimes we read in the New Testament the phrase "the church of God." Whether this descriptive phrase is present or not, however, it always is understood.

Most of the time, *ekklesia* in the New Testament denotes a local group of believers. Sometimes, as is true in Ephesians 1:15-23, all believers are included. Geography—that is, location—is not the important thing. The church is God's creation, and it belongs to him. This is what makes the church what it is. A person belongs to the church because he or she belongs to God, wherever that person may live.

Once again, in verse 23, a clause's major point is clear, but its precise meaning is difficult to determine. The clear point is: The church is the body of Christ.

This analogy is simply the flip side of the previous analogy. Christ is the head of the church; then by implication, the church is the body of Christ.

In their attempt to express the church's real meaning and nature, New Testament writers gave us many analogies for it. But of all the analogies, the Pauline concept of the church as Christ's body is perhaps the most influential today.

In the concept as used in Ephesians, the primary emphasis of the church as Christ's body seems to be on the lordship of Christ. He is Lord over all creation, but he is Lord over the church in a special sense; for the church is the community that joyfully and gratefully has come under his lordship and attempts to live according to his purpose.

The church's primary characteristic is its recognition of and response to Christ as Lord. Unfortunately, much of our ecclesiology fails to take this primary and crucial fact into consideration. Baptists have a congregational approach to church government. Out of this form of church government comes the concept that the church's decisions are based on the will of the majority. But when the majority decision is contrary to the Lord's will, as is sometimes the case, the church is not acting according to its nature as the body of Christ. The Bible shows us that the decision of the majority is sometimes the wrong decision. The Old Testament prophets are an example, for quite often they were alone in their perception of God's will. Also in the New Testament, Christian churches often took the wrong position, as is clear from such epistles as Galatians and 1 Corinthians.

If a church votes to exclude a person because of superficial considerations—such as class, race, or nationality—that church is defying the Lord's will. A church that excludes people generally justifies its stance on the basis of procedure. Then the church claims that it acted democratically; therefore, it must have made the right decision. An appeal to a political process, however, is no excuse for defying the Lord's will. Not the people's will, but the Lord's will must rule in the church's life.

An ambiguity occurs in the last part of verse 23. Two major possibilities exist. The Greek word translated "fulness" (KJV) can have an active or a passive meaning. The word can mean that Christ is doing the filling; or, the term can mean that Christ is the one being filled. In the former case, the phrase can mean: Christ who fills everything is also filling the church. In the latter case, it can mean: The church fills Christ so that he becomes totally full in every respect. If the second translation is correct, how are we to understand it? How can the church fill Christ so that he is totally full? The answer is that the church fills Christ by the incorporation of all members so that the body is whole.

Paul understood the church to be the body of Christ. But he also knew that the body was not complete at the moment that he wrote. Others were to be included. As long as the body lacks members, Christ is not full. Furthermore, Christ's body is not complete because it has to do a lot of growing in faith and love. This is a possible and logical meaning of Paul's thought in verse 23: Christ is being filled in the sense that his body is being filled as persons continue to become a part of it and as they continue to grow. If this interpretation is true, then it clarifies the church's mission. The body (church) rejoices in its relationship to its Lord; it grieves, however, over its own incompleteness. The body's goal is wholeness; its mission is to be the bearer of God's redemptive message, to be open and sensitive to those still outside the body, and to welcome all whom God calls to share in his new creation. The purpose of the church is to become as whole in its role as the body as the head of the church already is. When God accomplishes our wholeness as his people doing his redemptive work, his purpose will be achieved.

The Real Source of the Church's Strength

We live in an age dominated by the computer. People rush to join the latest popular movement as indicated by public opinion polls. The Gallup Poll and the Harris Poll periodically give us datum which indicate the present state of the church in American public opinion.

Unfortunately, many church members are influenced by the polls. Their optimism rises or wanes in light of the polls' latest reports. When Christianity is popular, many of us tend to feel that the church is going to prevail. When it begins to decline in popularity, we sometimes become gloomy about the prospects.

This kind of public-opinion-poll thinking expresses the world's mind, but not the mind illuminated by the Spirit. Our hope is not based on things that polls can measure and report. Our hope rests in what God has done and what he has promised he will do. We stubbornly must refuse to allow public opinion to affect our faith in God's church.

The church's power does not consist of the amount of money it can raise or the number of people it can attract to its banner. God's power, manifested in Jesus Christ, the church's Lord, is the basis for our confidence and hope. We need the "spirit of wisdom" for which Paul prayed (Eph. 1:17) so that we can grasp this truth.

---

1. From *The Jerusalem Bible* (Garden City, New York: Doubleday & Co., Inc., 1966), p. 331.

2. From *The New English Bible*. Copyright © The Delegates of the Oxford University Press and the Syndics of the Cambridge University Press, 1961, 1970. Reprinted by permission. Subsequent quotations are marked NEB.

Personal Learning Activities

1. To Paul, two attributes of a church were most important. Select the correct answers from the list:

   _____(1) Number of members

_____(2) Faith
_____(3) Buildings
_____(4) Love

2. According to Dr. Tolbert, _____ is one of the most basic of sins.
(Choose the proper response from the following list.)
(1) Dishonesty
(2) Covetousness
(3) Prejudice
(4) Jealousy

3. The name for God that emphasizes his relationship to believers as one
who loves them, cares for them, and meets their needs is (choose the
correct response):
_____(1) Lord of hosts
_____(2) Jehovah
_____(3) Father
_____(4) God Almighty

4. When Paul asked that God give his readers a spirit of wisdom, he
meant the ability to know a lot of facts. True _____ False_____

5. According to Dr. Tolbert, the goal of the Christian life is (select the
correct answer):
_____(1) To get to heaven
_____(2) To be free of difficulty
_____(3) To be successful
_____(4) To know God fully

6. For Paul, the _____ of Jesus Christ was the most crucial part of
the gospel. (Choose the proper response from the list.)
(1) Birth
(2) Preaching
(3) Resurrection
(4) Teaching

7. According to Paul, the secret of the church's victory is (choose the
correct response):
_____(1) A sophisticated program
_____(2) Human leadership
_____(3) Christ, the head
_____(4) A large budget

8. The church is (select the correct answers):
_____(1) The body of Christ
_____(2) An organization
_____(3) The people of God
_____(4) A democracy

Answers:
1. (2), (4); 2. (3); 3. (3); 4. False; 5. (4); 6. (3); 7. (3); 8. (1),
(3).

3

God's Power in the Lives of Believers

Ephesians 2:1-10

The Unbeliever's Hopeless Condition (2:1-3)

In Ephesians 1, the word "you" means *you Gentiles*. But in 2:1, the word "you" is placed in an emphatic position in the Greek text. So in 2:1 when Paul addressed himself first to his Gentile readers, the first thing he said about them was, *"You* were dead through the trespasses and sins."

The death to which Paul referred was not physical death, as is clear from Paul's description. Death is a metaphor for the existence of people who are alienated from God. Life is in God alone. Separation from God is death.

The cause of spiritual death is identified as "trespasses and sins" (v. 1). The singular of the word translated "trespasses" means a fall, hence a moral or spiritual failure. Although the word signifies a moral lapse, we must understand that what is involved is not of an impersonal nature. What is meant is not just the violation of a set of rules. As becomes clear later on, what is at stake is each person's relationship to God. Lapses or failures manifest problems; they are symptoms of the disease; they are indicative of something primary, basic. These lapses or failures express a fundamental rupture in a person's relationship to God. A person in sin, rebelling against God, expresses his or her rebellion by trespasses and sins.

The word for "sins" in the Greek text means missing a target or a road. Thus, the term could be used to describe intellectual errors or moral failures. The two words, *trespasses* and *sins,* are practical synonyms in our text. They describe the individual manifestations of unredeemed people's innate hostility against God.

Paul addressed the believers who had been dead spiritually. Verses 1-10 reflect Paul's fundamental salvation theology—the sinner without God is dead. He believed that salvation is something that lies outside the arena of human possibilities. To tell the sinner that he or she needs to begin living for God, to conform to laws, or any similar admonition is worse than useless. A person might as well tell a dead man that he needs to start breathing, to get up and move around. Therefore, the only answer to this human condition is a power beyond the individual who is involved in the situation. Such a person needs a resurrecting, lifegiving power. That power is God.

Sin not only causes the lost person's predicament, but sin also constitutes the environment in which his or her existence proceeds. But the word translated "once" (v. 2) emphasizes that this environment is no longer the context of the believer's life. Paul wanted his readers to know that they were no longer what they had been, for they had moved into a new sphere. Once they had "walked" in trespasses and sins. The verb "walked" in this context means "lived" and is translated in this manner in some recent versions.

The word *walk* encompasses attitudes, relationships, actions, goals—in short, all the ways in which a person expresses his or her being. In the unbeliever's life, all these ways of expressing being arise and occur in an atmosphere of hostility toward God. The whole environment is contaminated.

Furthermore, Paul taught that the existence of unbelievers in sin was a slave existence. They were under the control of an evil power. Their lives were determined by this evil power.

They walked, "following the course of this world" (v. 2). This rendering represents the translation of a difficult phrase. The term "course" translates the word *aiona,* which usually is rendered as age. *Aion* refers to a limited period of time. The English word derived from it is *aeon*.

In certain Hellenistic religious circles, however, *aion* came to be used as a god's name. Although the word usually is not personified in the New Testament, verse 2 seems to be an exception. Paul certainly was not thinking of the age of this world in a temporal sense. He had in mind a spiritual power that dominates sinners in this world age. Some translators, therefore, understand the phrase to mean spirit of this world.

The word "world" (*kosmos*) is used in various senses in the Bible, as it is in English. For example, we talk about the world of literature, my personal world, and the world of sports.

Lower Agora (Marketplace) in Ephesus. This was the scene of bustling activity in first-century Ephesus.

"This world" may mean the universe that God created, which the Bible affirms to be good. "This world" also can refer to humanity in its totality: "For God so loved the world" (John 3:16). But the "world" is also the arena in which people rebel against God. It is contaminated with evil. So the word *world* can be used to refer to the sphere that is dominated by sin and characterized by rebellion against God.

In the next phrase, Paul became more explicit. The sinner's way of life is determined by "the prince of the power of the air" (v. 2). Once again, although the essential meaning is clear, the exact thought in this phrase is difficult. We probably should equate this baleful and malignant power that Paul called a prince with Satan.

In this connection, we should note that Paul rarely referred to Satan or the devil. He preferred concepts like flesh or sin (singular), meaning the power that dominates people in their rebellion against God.

The ruler or "prince" (v. 2) is characterized as the one who possesses the authority of the air. In order to understand this description, we must know something of ancient cosmology and religion. In Paul's day, people commonly understood that the sphere between the earth and the stars was filled with impure air. Beyond lay the ethereal regions of purity and light.

The sphere of impure air was the place of abode for evil spirits or powers. Paul's phrase also implies the concept of an organized hierarchy of these evil powers under the domination of a prince or a ruler. The prince or ruler is the leader of those "spiritual hosts of wickedness in the heavenly places" about whom we read in Ephesians 6:12. *The New English Bible* translated the phrase: "When you obeyed the commander of the spiritual powers of the air" (2:2). This probably gives the sense of the phrase.

A third parallel phrase is present in the text. The evil power is described as "the spirit that is now at work in the sons of disobedience" (v. 2). "Sons of" in this usage is a Hebraism that means people who are characterized by a certain quality. The phrase "sons of disobedience" (v. 2) means disobedient or rebellious people.

Paul affirmed several things in the phrase, "sons of disobedience." This evil power or spirit still is working. The salvation event—centered in Jesus' resurrection—has not halted Satan's activity. In Jesus' resurrection, God demonstrated evil's eventual doom. Satan's hold over believers has been frustrated. This already has taken place. But evil is still a powerful, active force in the world. Paul's readers could verify that by just looking around. So can we.

Underlying Paul's phrase probably was the concept that Satan is a rebel against God. At any rate, rebellion is his work in human beings. Satan's power is active in the person who rebels against God.

Rebellion against God describes the human situation outside of redemption. Warfare exists between unredeemed people and God. Later in Ephesians, Paul emphasized that this warfare does not represent God's will and purpose. Incredibly, people rebel against their maker.

Rebellion against God is sin. People may lie, steal, and cheat. They may be arrogant, prejudiced, or cowardly. These actions and attitudes, however, do not constitute their central problem. These are only symptoms of their predicament. The source of people's primary problem is their alienation from God. People refusing God's grace are rebelling against the One to whom they owe their supreme allegiance. Their lives are not determined by the power of God, but by the power of evil.

For us to grasp this concept is crucial. Many people feel that they do not need the gospel because they are decent, honest, and trustworthy. I fear that our superficial concept of sin and the wrong ideas presented in our preaching and teaching may have led to this conclusion. Sometimes we hear people say: "Why should I be a believer? I am better than the deacons in your church." This statement may be true, but it is irrelevant. No sin is more serious than that expressed in the attitude: I do not need God. This is the essence of sin which is rebellion and alienation. The person who says, I do not need God, is the worst sinner of all, no matter how moral his life may be.

In Ephesians 2:1-2, Paul described the miserable, helpless plight of the idolatrous Gentiles. In verse 3, he placed the Jews in the same category. This is in keeping with the position he took in Romans 1—3 where he reached the conclusion that "all men, both Jews and Greeks, are under the power of sin" (Rom. 3:9).

In verse 3, Paul wrote "Among these we [Jews] all once lived." "Among these" probably refers to "the sons of disobedience" (v. 2). Here, Paul did not think of physical nearness. He meant that the Jews and Gentiles lived in the same spiritual sphere. They were citizens of the same realm, the realm of evil and death. Of course, the Jews he wrote about were the Christian Jews, as the word "once" indicates. God had taken the Jews, like the Gentiles, out of the sphere where death reigned and had placed them in the realm of life.

Paul declared that the lives of unbelieving Jews had been dictated by "the passions of our flesh" (v. 3). As in the English, "flesh" can have various meanings. The word can mean meat as well as human flesh. The term also can be used in the Hebraic sense of people in their weakness, finiteness, and distance from God. Paul, however, often used the term "flesh" to describe people in their rebellion against God. In this sense, the word is a practical equivalent of his use of the word *sin* to describe an evil power that is hostile to God and that dominates unregenerate humanity. This is the way "flesh" is employed here.

"Passions" (v. 3) translates a Greek word that often means desires. These desires may be good or bad. Here, however, the desires clearly are evil because they arise out of the flesh. The King James Version has the word "lusts," which gives an even stronger emphasis to the evil nature of these desires than does the Revised Standard Version's rendering "passions."

People dominated by the passions of the flesh do not live according to God's will. Rather, they follow "the desires of body and mind" (v. 3). "Desires" in this phrase translates a word that literally means wills. "Body" is the Revised Standard Version's rendering of the word *sarx* (flesh). Clearly, "body" is a better translation because flesh has a different meaning than in the previous context. The term "body" is joined with the word "mind." The willful decisions that determine the life of the unregenerate Jew came from flesh and thoughts. All of the unregenerate person is contaminated, therefore, from physical desires to the highest reaches of intellectual endeavors. As a result, Paul held that unbelieving Jews were "by nature children of wrath" just as were the pagan Gentiles (v. 3). This statement raises some difficult questions about the character and source of evil.

Some interpreters think Paul's statement indicates that he believed in original sin in the sense that evil is transmitted from parents to children in the process of birth. This understanding seems to do an injustice to Paul's thought. If he believed that people were helpless victims of evil because of inherited sin and guilt, why did he not write or talk about this? He did not say that they were condemned by original sin. He did say that they were "dead through the trespasses and sins" (Eph. 2:1). Their condition was the result of their own violations of God's will and not of their ancestors' sins.

When Paul described sin, he wrote about rebellious acts against God. He wrote about immorality and intellectual perversity. In other words, he discussed adult acts and attitudes. That Paul saw the rule of sin as universal and complete cannot be doubted seriously. This conclusion arose out of his observation of humanity's condition rather than out of an abstract doctrine of inherited guilt. His description of the human plight made this fact clear.

We must ask, What did Paul mean when he used the phrase "by nature" (v. 3)? The answer comes from his consciousness of the Jewish-Gentile controversy. He knew that his assessment of humanity's lost condition differed from that of his fellow, non-Christian Jews. They believed that Gentiles "by nature," because they were Gentiles, were alienated from God. However, they held that the situation was different for them. They had descended from Abraham, had received the law, and had been circumcised. By nature, they belonged to the people of God.

Paul refuted the Jews' fundamental assumption. He said that they were sinners just like the Gentiles because their rejection of God was just as real.

"Children of wrath" (v. 3) in this context is a Hebraism which means deserving of wrath. The phrase cannot mean objects of wrath. In the next passage, Paul showed that all of them, Jews and Gentiles, were objects of God's love and not wrath.

God's Solution to the Human Condition (2:4-7)

The stage now had been set for one of the greatest passages in the Bible. In the starkest and most realistic terms, Paul had described humanity's prevalent condition. Many persons were in the realm of death, rebels against God, without any possibility of extricating themselves, and deserving the punishment which would be expected from a holy God.

"But God . . . made us alive" (vv. 4-5). The English translation certainly catches the force of the transition. Paul introduced something new into the sorry scene that he had depicted. He introduced a new insight—God does not act as we might expect him to act. He does not move in vengeful fury to vent his anger on people who rebel against him. Sinners deserve his anger, but God does not respond in anger. No, instead of God's acting in anger, the opposite is true.

In verse 4, the first thing Paul wrote about God is the word that sinners desperately need to hear. That word is "mercy." The Hebrew equivalent of the New Testament word means God's steadfast love; love is an aspect of mercy. Another aspect of mercy is faithfulness. The sinner can depend on God's mercy, for it is not fitful, erratic, or subject to change.

God redeemed a people, established a covenant with them, and promised to relate to them in terms of that covenant. People often are unfaithful to God, unresponsive to his will, and hostile instead of loving. The opposite is true of God. He always can be counted on to be faithful in his love. In the New Testament, mercy can describe God's love in creating his people and his faithful, loving relationship to them after he creates them.

Paul described the scope of God's mercy when he wrote of God's being "rich in mercy" (v. 4). This is not miserly, inadequate, paltry mercy. Heaven knows, the sinner that Paul depicted cannot be helped by scanty mercy! But he does not have to worry about that. God's storehouse of mercy is replete; it is more than adequate to meet the sinner's needs. Paul put it in another letter, "Where sin increased, grace abounded all the more" (Rom. 5:20). Or, as Julia H. Johnston phrased it, we are met by "grace that is greater than all our sin."[1]

The Old Testament provides us with the word for mercy. The New Testament gives us the word for God's love. The term is *agape*. One of the major meanings of God's love is that he extends it to people who do not deserve it. This is the truth that Paul underlined in Ephesians 2:1-10. God loved us "when we were dead through our trespasses" (v. 5). As children of wrath, everyone deserved whatever judgment his or her trespasses called for; but while deserving wrath, all those open to God received love.

But all who responded to God needed more than love. We needed power. We were dead, helpless, incapable of coming back to life. But God has power! Life-giving power! He "made us alive together with Christ" (v. 5).

The two relationships involved in our resurrection are not clear in the English translation. First is our relationship with Christ. Our resurrection from the dead—our new life as God's people—is linked inextricably to Christ's resurrection. We are not made alive apart from Christ; our life comes through him and with him. This means that our life can be understood only in its solidarity with the life of the risen Lord.

Salvation is not some kind of soul insurance by which we escape hell and receive a mortgage on heaven. Redemption does not mean that we can make a decision and go on about our business. Not at all! From the moment of conversion, our life is bound indissolubly with Christ's life.

The second of the relationships is not made clear in the English translation. We not only are made alive with Christ. We also are made alive "together"—with other believers (v. 5). Paul knew nothing of an individual salvation in the way that many modern evangelicals think of it. Individual redemption has meaning only as it is a part of God's total redemptive work in creating the people of God. For a person to be converted and at the same time deny what God has done in the lives of fellow Christians is an abortion and not a birth. Birth brings a person into the family. Conversion brings one into God's family, God's new people.

At this point, Paul interpolated a thought into his discussion: "By grace you have been saved" (v. 5). He developed this idea in verses 8-9. Several points in the great statement engage our attention. For one thing, Paul switched abruptly from the first to the second personal pronoun. We know, however, that Paul believed his new life as well as that of his Gentile readers came about by grace.

The word "saved" was used in a way that was not characteristically Pauline. Normally, Paul would have written that believers *have been* justified, and they *will be* saved. In other contexts, Paul used salvation to refer to the believers' ultimate victory over the power of sin and death. (See Rom. 5:9; 13:11; 1 Cor. 5:5.) Moreover, the verb saved is perfect in Greek, as it is in the English translations. But in similar statements elsewhere, Paul used other tenses. However, the perfect tense is appropriate because it is used to describe something that happened in the past but whose effect continues into the present—and, we might add, into the future.

After the parenthetical statement, Paul picked up his train of thought. God "raised us up" (v. 6)—from the dead. He also "made us sit with him in the heavenly places" (v. 6). God's action in the believer's life parallels his action in Christ's life. God has given us new life and has exalted us to a

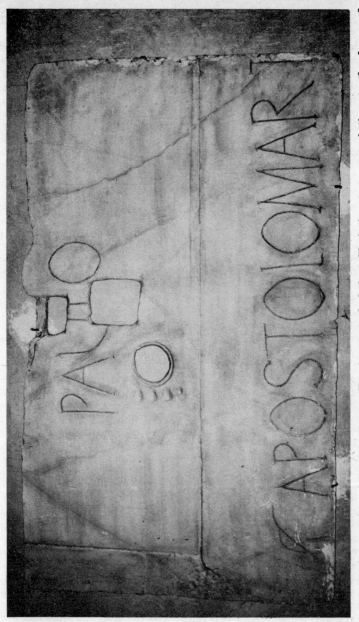

Traditional tomb of Paul in Rome. Paul contended that Christians are not victims to the force of death.

position of honor and power. The believer enters into a new sphere of existence called "the heavenly places." The Christian enters into this new sphere now, even while continuing life in this world. Paul was absolutely sure that the believer no longer was subject to the power of evil, no longer victim to the forces of death. The believer had been elevated above all those powers that sought the person's ruin and destruction.

All this takes place "in Christ Jesus" (v. 6). The Christian's victory cannot be separated from Christ's victory. Victory takes place because of Christ, through Christ, and in relation to Christ. What God did in Christ is indispensable for what he does in the believer.

Once again, the Revised Standard Version translation does not bring out emphatically a fundamental Pauline thought—we have been raised together and made to sit together. This is the sense of the Greek verbs. Ours is a co-resurrection and a co-elevation. Not only is triumph to be seen in association with Christ, but it is a victory that is shared with all other believers.

The epistle to the Ephesians emphasizes our salvation's present meaning more than the other Pauline epistles. To put it another way, in Paul's other letters he taught that salvation is more futuristic. But in Ephesians 2:7, the meaning of salvation is not exhausted in the present. Its fullness can be known only in the future, "in the coming ages."

The conception of time as a succession of ages is a Jewish idea. This idea differs radically from other concepts which view time in cycles. In a cyclical view of time, history is repetitious and without purpose. From the Jewish perspective, history has a purpose and is moving toward it through successive ages under the sovereign God's direction.

Whatever changes the ages may bring, however, the believer can be sure of one thing: God's attitude toward his child and God's actions on his child's behalf will not change. God will continue in his "kindness" or goodness (v. 7) to demonstrate to his children "the immeasurable riches of his grace."

One point is clear: Whatever God gives us and whatever he will give us is "grace," unmerited favor and love (v. 7). The time never will come when we can claim anything as our own because of our own merit. The time never will come when our relationship with God will not depend solely on his grace. Our salvation in its beginning was due to God's grace. Our present relationship with God is possible only through his grace. Our hope for the future is rooted in his grace; that is why it is a sure hope. We may waver and change, but God never changes. He is always a Father of grace.

A great truth for believers today emerges from Paul's confidence expressed in verse 7. Many of us have seen numerous changes in our lifetimes—a succession of ages, as it were. But whether the Christian lives under Hitler's fascist totalitarianism or Marx's leftist totalitarianism, one thing remains constant—God's grace.

Grace and Works (2:8-10)

In verse 8, Paul returned to the affirmation introduced in verse 5, but he added another idea. We have been saved by grace "through faith." We might add *only* through faith, for this was Paul's conviction.

Faith is the individual's response to God's grace. As Jesus was fond of teaching, faith is a little child's attitude toward a loving father. The little child is totally dependent, totally vulnerable, totally helpless. Yet the child lives without fear in this vulnerability because of complete confidence in a strong and loving father.

Faith, then, arises out of an awareness of our helplessness. Faith responds to a loving, gracious Father in terms of trust and makes the Father's love the sole guarantee of the future. Not money, not power, not prestige, not weapons, but a strong Father's grace is the genuine believer's security.

In the first part of verse 8, Paul stated his conviction about the believer's relationship to God. In order to make sure that his idea was clear, he stated it negatively in the last part of the verse: "This is not your own doing."

Some question exists among interpreters about the antecedent of "this." Does it refer to grace or to faith? Or does it refer to the whole statement? In Greek, the demonstrative pronoun for "this" is neuter in gender, while grace and faith are feminine. Because of this difference in gender, the grammar seems to indicate that Paul referred to the whole preceding idea when he used "this." Salvation by grace through faith is in no sense a human achievement.

Whatever one makes of the grammar, the reason for Paul's statement is clear. Salvation by faith is the opposite of, and excludes, any notion of salvation by works.

To be sure, people can, and often do, make faith a human work. When do we know that faith has been made a work? We know that what we call faith has become a human work if we are arrogant because we believe or if we are contemptuous of others because they do not believe. This attitude cannot be produced by the kind of faith Paul wrote about.

Pride and faith are incongruous (v. 9). Paul saw that these attitudes were mutually exclusive. We need to recognize this truth, too. Works produce boasting; faith eliminates boasting. This recognition is the key. Our salvation from start-to-finish is an expression of God's grace. As James M. Gray phrased it:

> *Naught have I gotten*
> *but what I received;*
> *Grace hath bestowed it*
> *Since I have believed.*

To conclude from Paul's proclamation of a gospel of grace that he was contemptuous of good works is wrong and dangerous. Earlier, some members of the church reached this erroneous conclusion. They taught that good works had no place in a gospel of grace, for it did not matter what a person did. From this point of view, grace covers all our sins; so, it does not matter how much we sin. The people who held this view believed that grace relieved Christians of all responsibility in doing anything. We call this doctrine libertinism. This teaching stands at the opposite pole from legalism, which contends that what people do is the only important thing. Legalism contends that people are saved or lost as a result of their works.

Paul was not against good works. He was against legalism. He opposed the idea that we are saved by our performance. But he was also against libertinism. He did not believe grace meant that human beings are irresponsible. Quite the reverse is true. From Paul's point of view, grace freed people to be responsible. Prior to their conversion, in their slave-existence, responsible relationships to God were impossible. As Paul wrote in Romans, "Those who are in the flesh cannot please God" (Rom. 8:8). People can live in a way that pleases God only after they are released from their condition as slaves to wrong.

Paul made clear his conviction that grace is prior to good works and that the believer is not saved by good works. He did this in the statement: "For we are his workmanship, created in Christ Jesus" (v. 10). The English text hardly can give the emphasis that the Greek syntax does. Literally, we could translate the phrase to say, *of him* we are a workmanship. One must stress the possessive pronoun "his" in the English translation in order to bring out the flavor of the Greek text where "his" is in the first or emphatic position. That is, the emphasis is on God and on the fact that the believing community exists only through his gracious work, his creative activity.

Good works do not bring the believer into being as God's child. God's act of redemption stands prior to anything the believer does. What the Christian does, he does as God's child and not in order to become God's child.

Note another point before we continue. In this Scripture text, an important aspect of the church stands out clearly. The church is God's creation. We speak of organizing, establishing, or founding churches. This language is not true to the New Testament concept of the church. Our common words are antithetical to the New Testament concept, for such phrases imply that a church comes into existence as a result of human endeavor or works. This idea is the exact opposite of Paul's position.

God created us for a purpose—to love and serve him. As Paul wrote it, the believing community was created "for good works" (v. 10). These works, however, are not human good works. The accomplishments are not defined or chosen by people; rather, they are those which "God prepared beforehand." The doing of God's good works means that the believer becomes a responsible participant in the eternal plan of redemption.

The good works designed by God were defined more specifically by Paul in subsequent passages of Ephesians. The main point to be made, however, is that Paul understood the believer's life and works in terms of God's revelation of himself and his plan in Jesus Christ.

A central aspect of God's plan, as we have seen, is his victory over the divisive forces which tear his world apart. Bringing together Jew and Gentile into one body was fundamental to God's plan of redemption. In the light of this truth, Paul wrote in Ephesians about one fundamental aspect of the believer's life or walk. The Christian was to accept all people whom God accepted. The believer was to live in love in a responsible relationship with others. One good work God has prepared beforehand for us to walk (live) in is to establish and maintain bonds of fellowship.

Paul's View and Ours

Paul had been an enemy of God's redemptive plan in Jesus Christ. His readers had been immersed in the immorality and idolatry of a pagan world. Paul knew what grace meant. Only because God had loved him when he was perverse and disobedient had his salvation become a reality.

Perhaps many of us do not have a real sense of what being lost means. We use terms like lost, dead in sin, and rebels against God. But do these terms have real meaning for us? If they do not have real meaning, can grace have the significance it ought to have?

Perhaps the lack of a real understanding of lostness explains why many of us are not as willing to suffer, work, and even die to proclaim the gospel of grace as Paul was. Perhaps this lack of understanding explains our selfishness and complacency, our poor and weak commitment to the church's mission, and our lack of personal commitment to our Lord.

---

1. Words, Julia H. Johnston, 1910. Copyright 1910. Renewal 1936 extended. Hope Publishing Co., owner. All rights reserved. Used by permission.

Personal Learning Activities

1. Match the two lists, linking term with definition:

_____(1) Trespass   (a) Rebellious people
_____(2) Sin   (b) Sphere dominated by sin
_____(3) Walk   (c) A falling
_____(4) World   (d) All the ways one expresses being
_____(5) Sons of disobedience   (e) Missing the mark

2. Paul probably equated the "prince of the power of the air" with Satan.
   True _____ False _____
3. The term Paul characteristically used to describe people in their rebellion against God was (choose the proper response):
   _____(1) Wrong
   _____(2) Pagan
   _____(3) Flesh
   _____(4) Mistaken
4. Paul used the phrase "by nature children of wrath" to emphasize God's anger at people who were sinners from birth. True _____ False _____
5. The word _____ has behind it the Old Testament concept of God's steadfast love. (Select the correct answer from the following list.)
   (1) Compassion
   (2) Righteousness
   (3) Mercy
   (4) Power
6. Paul was contemptuous of good works, even after a person's conversion.
   True _____ False _____
7. According to Dr. Tolbert, God created us for a purpose. From the following list, select the suggested purpose.
   _____(1) To enjoy life
   _____(2) To love and serve God
   _____(3) To be prosperous
   _____(4) To be well liked

Warning stone in the Temple in Jerusalem. This stone warned Gentiles not to go beyond the court of the Gentiles in the Temple.

4

The Inclusion of the Gentiles

Ephesians 2:11-22

In his previous discussion, Paul had implied that a new relationship existed among those who had been objects of God's saving love. Both Jews and Gentiles had been in the same situation—that is, in a state of rebellion against God. Both had been dead in their sins, and both had been under the dominion of hostile, evil powers.

God, however, had saved Jews and Gentiles who had responded to the gospel. These converts were the centerpiece of God's redemptive plan to unite a fragmented universe. They had been raised *together* in the heavenly places in Christ Jesus. This implies that God had established a new community of redeemed people.

In Ephesians 2:11-22, Paul became more explicit. He declared expressly that the former state of alienation between Gentiles and Israel, the covenant community, had been overcome.

Paul presented the division of the world from the Jewish perspective. Paul believed that God's grace also had caused other divisions to be transcended (Gal. 3:28). But in Ephesians, he was concerned with the Jewish concept of the world. Rightly understood, this Jewish concept represented Paul's view and, indeed, the biblical view. Paul divided the world into God's people and those who were outside his people—the Gentiles, the nations, or the pagans. The Greek word can be translated in all three ways.

For Paul, this was a genuine division. To be sure, some had superficial, erroneous, and sinful perceptions of this division. These false perceptions arose from the prejudiced Jews who did not understand that birth, circumcision, and possession of the law did not mean that one actually belonged to God's people.

Whatever the Jews' prejudices and hostilities toward Gentiles, the latter indeed had been outside the community of faith. They had not been in the stream of God's revelatory and redemptive activity as this activity is depicted in the Old Testament.

The Alienation of the Gentiles (2:11-12)

At the beginning of Paul's exposition, he enjoined his non-Jewish readers to "remember" their former state (v. 11). The verb "remember" in verse 11 implies to recollect or reflect; it also involves an appropriate response in terms of attitudes and actions. At the very least, to remember in biblical usage includes worship and praise. Furthermore, remembering can elicit actions appropriate to God's great blessings. Also, appropriate remembering can result in changed or improved lives.

Paul called on his Gentile readers to remember what they had been formerly. They had been pagans, idol worshipers. He described them first of all as "Gentiles in the flesh" (v. 11). A question always arises when we come across the term "flesh" in Paul's writings. Did "flesh" refer to the realm of hostility and rebellion against God, as it so often does? Once, the Gentiles belonged to this realm of existence, as Paul described in 2:1-2.

In verse 11, "in the flesh" probably referred to the physical manifestations of the readers' Gentile status. From this point of view, they still could be called "Gentiles in the flesh" because they were uncircumcised. This superficial, external manifestation indicated that they were not Jews. But Paul believed that this physical aspect was superficial, as is seen in his statement about calling them Gentiles. The Gentiles were called "the uncircumcision" (v. 11); their Jewish contemporaries referred to them in this derogatory manner.

"Uncircumcision" in the Jewish vocabulary was a word of contempt and derision. It was like all words which have to do with external appearances or circumstances with which some people put down others. The contempt and arrogance of such terms are a manifestation of sin's pervasive power.

The Jews who called Gentiles "the uncircumcision" called themselves "the circumcision." This superficial outward badge of their Jewishness was "made in the flesh by hands" (v. 11). A number of things are implied. (1) Idols are made by human hands. (2) Circumcision had become an idol. (3) Jews who trusted in circumcision believed that what people did was decisive rather than what God did.

From Paul's point of view, a circumcision and an uncircumcision existed that were important (Rom. 2:25-29). These had nothing to do with a person's physical appearance. They had to do with the heart. People who turned to God by faith were the circumcision. Those who rejected him belonged to the uncircumcision, whether they were circumcised physically or not.

In verse 12, Paul moved from the superficial to the Gentiles' genuine problem. In the past, they were "separated from Christ"—the Messiah. They were not part of that community of faith to whom God first revealed his redemptive purpose in the Messiah. In the past, God gave his prophets glimpses of his future. But the Gentiles did not share their expectations.

Second, the Gentiles had been excluded from citizenship in "the commonwealth of Israel." As the *Today's English Version* translates the idea, Gentiles were "foreigners."[1]

The word "commonwealth" used by the Revised Standard Version's translators has connotations of geography and political organization. But membership in the covenant community did not depend on these. Israelites were Israelites whether they lived in Palestine or not.

For Paul, Israel was the covenant community in both the Old Testament and the New Testament. In the New Testament, the covenant community is the church. But Paul believed that a people of God had existed before Christ that was determined by faith and obedience, not by physical circumcision. Gentiles had not been a part of this community.

Furthermore, the Gentiles had been "strangers to the covenants" based on the promise (v. 12). The covenants had expressed a gracious God's desire for fellowship with his people. The covenants constituted the basis of Israel's life. The key concept in Ephesians 2:12 is contained in the singular "promise," perhaps because for Paul all of God's promises were included in the one promise of a coming Messiah.

The Gentiles had been ignorant of God's dealings with the Israelites. The Gentiles had lived outside of his redemptive activity. They had not lived by faith in a God who fulfills his promise. Moreover, they did not have "hope" (v. 12). This does not refer to the subjective experience of hope, for Gentiles had their hopes and expectations. But whatever hopes they had were baseless and doomed to frustration.

The Gentiles did not have the hope of which people never will be ashamed. The one valid hope is the hope that rests in God. Biblical hope is not sentimental longing for a utopia or a baseless expectation that things are going to turn out better. Hope in the New Testament is confidence in a God who already has revealed his power and love in human history. In Israel, God's power and love had been displayed in the Exodus, in the wilderness wanderings, and in other manifestations. Later God revealed, through the resurrection of the Messiah, that he is worthy of hope. Until this time, the Gentiles had not possessed this hope in a God who acts to redeem his people.

Finally, the Gentiles were "without God" (v. 12). Our English word *atheist* is derived from the word translated "without God." For us, an "atheist" is one who does not believe in any God at all. In the ancient world, this was not generally true. For the most part, Gentiles believed in many gods. Yet, they were godless in the sense that they were without the one, true, and living God.

The Gentiles were without God "in the world" (v. 12). Does "world" mean this physical universe, created by God? If so, Paul's statement has a pathetic, poignant ring. The words describe the hopeless, miserable plight of the person who lives in God's world alone, bereft of the companionship of him who made it.

The person without God in the world may have much of the world's goods, but that person is poverty-stricken. This one may have much of the world's power, but he or she is helpless. To be alone in the world without God is the most pathetic, pitiable condition in which a person can be. Such a person has no ultimate reason for existence, no hope that lies beyond the here and now.

"World" also may have the same meaning as flesh. To be in the world— under its power, determined by its customs and goals—is the same as being without God. We cannot be sure which of these ideas was paramount in Paul's mind when he wrote the phrase.

The Broken Wall (2:13-18)

Paul called on his readers to "remember"—that is, to celebrate in praise and adoration, in commitment and service, what God had done for them. God had delivered them from their condition of hopelessness and alienation. They could celebrate because of the radical change in their existence. That change was heralded by the opening words of verse 13—"But now." "Now" stands in contrast to "at that time" of verse 12.

The next phrase, "in Christ Jesus," stands in contrast to "separated from Christ," also in verse 12. In verse 13, the emphasis is solely on God's gracious action on behalf of the Gentile Christians. The problem of distance, of alienation, of being an outsider was not overcome by anything within those erstwhile, excluded aliens. Because they were "in Christ," they had been brought near to God's people. In Christ they were no longer aliens, but they were "fellow citizens with the saints" (Eph. 2:19).

God's inclusion of the Gentiles in his people was made possible through the great saving event: Jesus' death on the cross. Thus, Paul could say that the Gentiles had been brought near "in the blood of [the] Christ [the Messiah]" (v. 13), which is the same as saying that their alienation had been resolved by or through the Messiah's death.

The Inclusion of the Gentiles

Now we come to the key passage in the whole epistle. In th[...] Paul defined more clearly the role of the Messiah in overcom[...] distance between Jew and Gentile. He also described the results o[...] Messiah's work when he wrote about the church, the new community created by God through Christ. In this community, the old divisions have been transcended; and God's goal of unity has been achieved.

Paul began with the strongest possible affirmation about the role of Christ (Messiah). He did not say that Christ produces, brings about, or causes peace to take place. Rather, Paul affirmed boldly, "He is our peace" (v. 14). The pronoun "he" at the beginning of verse 14 is emphatic, a fact that is not brought out in many of our translations. We translate it correctly if we say, He himself (or he in his own person) is our peace.

"Peace" does not mean merely the cessation of hostilities, an interlude in the never-ending wars of the world, although this was its common meaning in non-biblical Greek. The word's meaning in the text is determined by its biblical antecedents. In the Old Testament, *shalom* (peace) often was used to describe an existence of security and well-being that God brings about. In some contexts, it is the equivalent of salvation.

Paul certainly thought about salvation when he used the word "peace" in verse 13. At this point, he was concerned about its meaning in terms of the new relationship that Christians have with each other. Later on, he wrote about people's new relationship to God, which is also a relationship of peace. The former is a function of the latter. Peace between people and God means peace between persons who have been reconciled to God. In this Ephesians passage, the order was determined by Paul's immediate purpose rather than by the demands of logical theological exposition.

Many arguments have been advanced about the personal versus the social gospel. These arguments tend to divide what is not divided in the New Testament. A right personal relationship with God involves as a necessary element a right relationship with others. In a sense, we can say that the good news is only social: The gospel has to do only with relationships from beginning to end—relationship to God and relationships among his people.

When Paul used the word "peace," he had in mind a new relationship both to God and to others. The emphasis may vary, but the one presupposes the other in every case. This emphasis on relationship to God and to people is why a church which closes its doors to people because of race, class, or any reason other than a gospel consideration is a contradiction. Exclusion is an evidence of the gospel's failure rather than its success. Exclusion contradicts the New Testament teaching because such action says that God does not do what he teaches. (See Gal. 2:11-14.)

What is meant by the affirmation, "He is our peace" (v. 14)? The statement emphasizes what we have been examining. Peace is not the result of something we do or do not do; it is not brought about by living according to

...nd in the person of Christ. The way we come to
...through our relationship to him.

...e and hostility does not come about through the
...as so many believe today. Education's failure to
...a be attested through an examination of the rela-
...le in any department of a major university. People
...rees do not have less hostility and contempt than
...ch that level of education. They have at least as much,
...y have more hostility and contempt.

...weeping affirmation, Paul went on to give the reasons
why ...peace. The first reason is negative. Christ has done away
with that wh... divided people. Paul referred to this dividing element in
three ways, all of which apparently are synonymous.

Paul called the dividing element the "dividing wall" that separated Jew
from Gentile ("the middle wall of partition," v. 14, KJV), the hostility
(v. 14), and the law of commandments and ordinances (v. 15). The Revised
Standard Version's translation obscures the fact that wall, hostility, and
law of commandments are in apposition to one another in the Greek text.

Many suggestions have been made about the possible source for Paul's
thinking when he used the figure of a wall. Of course, literal walls
abounded in the ancient world, as they do in the modern world.

A wall or balustrade in the Temple divided the Court of the Gentiles from
the area to which only Jews were permitted access. On this wall, notices
were written warning Gentiles that they were not to go beyond that point
on penalty of death. The accusation against Paul in Acts 21:28b was that
he had taken Trophimus, a Gentile, into the forbidden area of the Temple
complex.

Even within the area permitted to Jews, barriers existed. Women could
not go beyond the Court of Women. Male Israelites could not go beyond the
Court of Israel. Only priests could enter the Court of the Priests and the
sanctuary. But the sanctuary proper was divided by a veil beyond which
only the high priest could go, and then only on the Day of Atonement (*Yom
Kippur*). When he wrote "dividing wall" (v. 14), Paul may have had in
mind the abolition or destruction of the wall which excluded Gentiles. Or,
he may have thought of the veil in the sanctuary that symbolized the
distance between man and God.

But "wall" is such a logical metaphor for the hostilities and prejudices
which divide people that probably no specific wall was in Paul's mind. Our
world, of course, has its dividing walls, such as the Berlin Wall. But even
where no concrete barriers are evident, walls exist wherever people live.
They are constructed of suspicion, misunderstanding, fear, prejudice, and
hatred.

Paul stated that Christ broke down the dividing wall. Further, Christ
destroyed the "hostility" (v. 14). Hostility may have been personified here,

as Paul personified sin and flesh in other contexts. He may have had in view an evil, oppressive power that holds people in its grip. Of course, Paul had in mind the active, personal enmity between Jews and Gentiles. The history of their relationships had been one of hostility, augmented through the centuries by periodic acts of violence. They hated each other passionately. But the wonder of the gospel was that it destroyed this hatred and put love in its place.

Paul further defined hostility by putting it in apposition to "the law of commandments and ordinances" (v. 15). This phrase is difficult to interpret. In other contexts, Paul taught that Christ did not destroy the law, rather, that he established or upheld it. (See Rom. 3:31.) How are we to understand the phrase here in Ephesians? We probably should begin by noting that Paul qualified the word *law* by the phrase, commandments [consisting] in ordinances [statutes]. This is a better translation of the Greek text than the Revised Standard Version's translation "commandments and ordinances." Probably in perspective here is the way Jews used the individual statutes of the law in order to justify their exclusiveness. The law indeed had become a wall separating the Jewish and Gentile worlds.

In their oral traditions, the Jews had built a fence around the law. Multitudes of rulings or ordinances arose that governed such things as sabbath observance. They were building the wall higher and higher. Paul, a Pharisee, had been nurtured in this way of life, and he had dedicated himself to destroying the Christian community in order to protect the way of life based on ordinances.

Jesus destroyed this way of using or understanding the law. Today, some of Jesus' followers continue to use the Bible in the ways Jews used the law. On the basis of individual interpretations and practices, they build fences around themselves. They forget what Paul emphasized in Ephesians: Relationship is important, not ordinances. Indeed, the possibility of peace through relationship had destroyed the way of the law as a means of salvation.

The destruction of the barrier was accomplished "in his flesh" (v. 15). This phrase is synonymous with "the blood of Christ" (v. 13) and "the cross" (v. 16). In his incarnation, Jesus came to grips with the evil powers and destroyed them.

Paul stated the work of the Messiah negatively: He destroyed the enmity. Paul then stated the Messiah's work positively: Christ's purpose is to "create in himself one new man in place of the two" (v. 15). The verb is "create," not "make." The church was not organized or founded by people. The church was created by God through Christ. The "new man" is the new race, God's new people. As Paul wrote in an earlier epistle, "There is neither Jew nor Greek, there is neither slave nor free, there is neither male nor female; for you are all one in Christ Jesus" (Gal. 3:28).

With this creation, a new age—the last age—has begun. God's purpose of unity for the race had been destroyed by sin. As a consequence, alienation became the order of the day. For Paul, the hostility between Jew and Gentile was an expression of the alienation which thwarted God's purpose of unity. But in his new act of creation, God had expressed his eternal purpose. God's power is greater than the power of evil. The age-old divisions of humanity are resolved in his new and mighty act of creation.

A twisted kind of theology makes God the author of the world's divisions. This is perverse theology, for it turns everything upside down. God becomes Satan, and Satan becomes God, in that Satan's purpose and work are attributed to God. Paul understood that God's purpose is to break down the walls built up by people under sin's power. God's purpose certainly does not include raising up those walls.

Christ did away with the barrier which separated Jews and Gentiles in order that he "might reconcile us both to God" (v. 16). The point primarily is the bringing together of disparate and hostile elements of humanity in the act of reconciliation. Christ did not reconcile the Jews to God apart from the Gentiles, nor did he reconcile the Gentiles separately from the Jews. Simultaneously, God's work of reconciliation has both vertical and horizontal dimensions. Reconciliation is at one and the same time with God and with other people. All who come to God must come to God together.

As Paul understood the church, it has moved out of the pagan structures of race, politics, and social class. It has transcended all the old animosities and arrogances. This reconciliation of Gentiles and Jews to God takes place "in one body" (v. 16). "Body" evidently refers to the church as the body of Christ. This is a figure which Paul discussed later in the epistle (4:15-16). The figure was introduced in earlier letters with different emphases. (See Rom. 12:4-8; 1 Cor. 12:12-27.)

Ephesians 2:17 is a reference to the public ministry of Jesus the Messiah. It contains a quotation from Isaiah 57:19. This quotation was one way of indicating that Jesus fulfilled the messianic expectations of the Old Testament as God's messenger of peace.

But Christ was not only the proclaimer of God's peace or salvation. He is the instrument through whom peace becomes a reality. This truth is declared in verse 18. Through him "we both," Jew and Gentile, "have access in one Spirit to the Father."

In 2:18, Paul wrote about worship. The office of priest has become unnecessary through the fulfilling and ultimate priestly role of Christ. Through him, people now approach God. No limiting barriers stand in the sanctuary. All believers can go beyond the veil through Christ. Worship of God is immediate, direct, and personal.

Paul further qualified this access: It is "in (or by) one Spirit" (v. 18). "Spirit" probably refers to God's Spirit. The emphasis is on *one*. One Spirit is present dynamically in Jewish and Gentile believers, not two or three Spirits. The Spirit is the unifying power operating in the church. The church is bound together by its experience of the Spirit and by the Spirit's action in its life.

No developed doctrine of the Trinity as such occurs in the New Testament. However, from passages like Ephesians 2:11-22, Christians later developed their Trinitarian formulations.

God's New Temple (2:19-22)

Paul returned to develop the idea introduced in verse 13 in order to give additional thoughts on the meaning of the church. "Strangers and sojourners" (v. 19) described two alien groups in Israel. The first term often was used to designate the visiting alien. The second word frequently was used of those outsiders who settled down and made their homes in Israelite territory. What Paul meant was that such terminology no longer applied in the church. No such thing as an outsider exists.

All Gentile believers are "fellow citizens with the saints" (v. 19)—the people who belong to God. All are members of the commonwealth of Israel. This phrase contains political terminology. The following phrase has the terminology of the family. All are "members of the household of God" (v. 19). All believers are brothers and sisters, belonging to a family whose head or Father is God.

From social terminology, Paul moved to the idea of a building to describe the church. The church is "built upon the foundation of the apostles and prophets" (v. 20). The "apostles" were the living witnesses to their personal knowledge about Christ's resurrection. Without their witness, the church would not have come into being. "Prophets" probably refers to Christian preachers. The prophets were the people who proclaimed God's word to the churches. Through them, God revealed his will about new decisions, new actions, and new attitudes necessary to cope with the ever-changing challenges and questions that confronted the church.

In another context, Paul wrote that Jesus Christ is the foundation of the church (1 Cor. 3:11). However, in Ephesians 2:20, he used a different metaphor. He did so because the emphasis was on unity. Therefore, he wrote that Jesus Christ is the "cornerstone" or, perhaps better, keystone (v. 20). This keystone was the final stone placed in the building, probably set over the gate. It locked the whole building into place, kept it from falling, and preserved its integrity. Jesus is the keystone that completes the church and gives unity and permanence to it.

In verse 21, Paul made clear the kind of building he had in mind. It is a "holy temple," a place for the worship of God. Some have said that Paul desacralized the holy places. For Paul, no buildings were holy, no man-made structures were sanctuaries. God's temple is a person (1 Cor. 6:19) or the church—God's people. (See also 1 Cor. 3:16.)

In Christ, the temple is built or joined together. The image in verse 21 is that of shaping and placing the stones so that they make a harmonious whole. Paul also said that in Christ this structure "grows" into a temple (v. 21). Paul knew well that the church was not a finished work. He wrote about this truth later in Ephesians. The church still is incomplete because other stones are to be added to it. But Paul had confidence that it will be completed, for the work is God's work.

In verse 22, Paul stated the purpose of the temple. It is "a dwelling place of God in the Spirit." It is a temple of the Holy Spirit, as Paul wrote in 1 Corinthians 3:16. The primary meaning of the Holy Spirit is elucidated by this statement. The Holy Spirit is God present with his people. The Holy Spirit's presence is the sign that the church is really the church. The church cannot exist apart from the Holy Spirit.

Once again, we need to recognize that Paul's primary concern was the concept of unity. The Revised Standard Version's translation "built" in verse 22 does not do justice to the Greek compound verb or to its tense, which is the present. Literally, believers are being built *together* into a dwelling place of the Spirit. The process of building is ongoing. The process involves all believers. Paul knew nothing about a private religion or private Christian development. All Christian growth takes place in the fellowship of the church.

God's Continuing Work

A pervasive tendency in society today is to deprecate the church. Some of this deprecation reflects a distaste for organization of any kind—as if organization could be avoided in human society. This tendency also reflects an emphasis on an inward, personal interpretation of religion.

Some people say, "I can worship God as well or better by myself. I do not need the church." Such an attitude stands at the other pole from Paul's view expressed in Ephesians 2:11-22. One just as well might say that a bunch of stones lying on the ground do not need each other to make a building.

God's ultimate purpose is not to create individual stones. His purpose is to put the stones together to form a living and eternal temple.

Modern churches spend much of their time, energy, and resources erecting buildings. This feverish construction is interesting, because the emphasis in the New Testament is on the body of Christ that meets in the building. We need to examine our activities to determine if they are necessary for the modern church's function and if they are pleasing to God. Otherwise, our efforts are misspent to a great extent.

We learn from the New Testament that God is interested in putting his people together to form one new humanity. This is where our emphasis and effort must be directed. The building up of the body of Christ in faith and love is a primary activity of God's Spirit, and the work of building up should be one of our major concerns.

To build buildings of stone and mortar is easier than to allow God to use us to build his temple. In order for God to do his work, we have to allow his Spirit to deal with our pride and prejudice. You see, we have to be willing to allow God to fit us in among all those other living stones. We cannot choose the building blocks. That choice is the work of God.

------

1. This quotation is from *The Bible in Today's English Version*. Old Testament: Copyright © American Bible Society 1976. New Testament: Copyright © American Bible Society 1966, 1971, 1976. Used by permission. Subsequent quotations are marked (TEV).

Personal Learning Activities

1. Paul divided the world into two broad divisions. Select the answer containing those divisions from the following list.
   _____(1) Rich and poor
   _____(2) Wise and unintelligent
   _____(3) Jew and Gentile
   _____(4) Male and female
2. In the New Testament, hope usually means wishful thinking. True _____ False _____
3. In Paul's statement, "He (Christ) is our peace," the word "peace" means (choose the proper response from the list):
   _____(1) Cessation of hostilities among nations
   _____(2) An end to personal differences
   _____(3) Well being brought about by God, salvation
4. Dr. Tolbert understands Paul's phrase "dividing wall" to have behind it (choose the correct answer from the list):
   _____(1) A barrier in the Temple
   _____(2) A stone fence

_____(3) A wall in a house

_____(4) No specific wall, but hostility and prejudice

5. In Ephesians 2:15, the phrase "new man" means (select the proper response from the list):

_____(1) A new person

_____(2) The new race, new people of God

_____(3) A reformed individual

6. To Paul, "reconciliation" meant relating to God, but not necessarily relating to people. True_____ False_____

7. For Paul, God's holy Temple is (choose the proper answer from the list):

_____(1) A future structure

_____(2) The new people of God

_____(3) A church building

Answers:
1. (3); 2. False; 3. (3); 4. (4); 5. (2); 6. False; 7. (2)

Model of Herod's Temple. The large area to the right is the court of the Gentiles. The low wall had warning stones placed in it.

5

Paul, Apostle to the Gentiles

Ephesians 3:1-13

A Prisoner for the Gentiles (3:1)

Ephesians 3:1-13 begins with a personal reference probably alluding to Paul's own situation at the time he wrote the letter. He described himself as "a prisoner for Christ Jesus on behalf of [for the sake of] you Gentiles." Further on in the passage, Paul also referred to his suffering for his readers (3:13). From these remarks, interpreters have assumed that Ephesians was written from prison. Many people also believe that Paul's imprisonment was in Rome, although Ephesians gives us no help on this matter. If these conclusions are correct, Paul's earlier letters (especially 2 Cor. 8—9; Rom. 15) and Acts 20—28 help us to understand why Paul referred to his imprisonment as he did in Ephesians.

During the closing years of his ministry in the Middle East, Paul had engaged actively in raising an offering for the impoverished Jewish believers in Judea. (See 1 Cor. 16:1; 2 Cor. 8—9; Rom. 15.) He had had high hopes for this offering. It could relieve physical suffering; also, it could help tear down the wall of hostility between Jewish and Gentile Christians. By giving the offering, Gentiles would acknowledge their debt to their Jewish brothers. (See Rom. 15:26-27.) The gospel had come to them through the Jews. By receiving the offering, Jewish believers would rec-

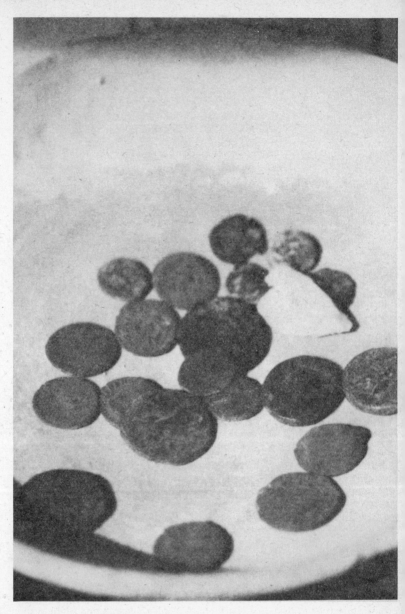

Roman coins of the first century A.D.

ognize the presence of God's surpassing grace which was the reason for their Gentile brothers' love and concern. (See 2 Cor. 9:12-14.)

For Paul, continued prejudice and hostility between Jews and Gentiles in the Christian community blatantly contradicted the gospel. To deal with this problem, therefore, was extremely inportant.

When the time came to transport the offering to the Jewish Christians, Paul decided to go with the group charged with this responsibility. He made this decision even though it would mean a long delay for his plans to evangelize the Roman province of Spain. Furthermore, he was aware that he would be risking his life. His decision to go to Jerusalem shows how much relations between Jewish and Gentile Christians meant to him.

After Paul arrived in Jerusalem, he was mobbed in the Temple. Some Jews from Asia accused him of taking Trophimus, a Gentile, into the forbidden precinct of the Temple. (See Acts 21:27-29.) If the Roman soldiers had not intervened promptly, Paul would have been lynched.

The point is this: All the Jewish hostility was directed toward Paul because he, a Jew, preached that Gentiles were included in God's redemptive plan on equal footing with Jews. Paul was considered a Jewish renegade, a traitor to the traditions in which he had been reared.

From Jerusalem, Paul was transported to Caesarea where he stayed two years. From Caesarea, he was taken to Rome where Ephesians probably was written.

The preceding information furnishes a background for Paul's description of himself in Ephesians 3:1. He was a prisoner on behalf of the Gentiles. His imprisonment was a result of his preaching the gospel to Gentiles. He was willing to pay any price in order to be God's instrument in evangelizing them. The Roman authorities imprisoned his body, but he really was not their prisoner. He was "a prisoner for Christ Jesus." Jesus had captured him, body and spirit. He owned no other master. If Christ had not owned Paul, Paul would not have been a Roman prisoner when he wrote Ephesians.

Jesus captured Paul for a purpose—to make Paul the channel through which God's redemptive love could reach out to the pagan world. This may be what Paul meant when he described himself as "a prisoner for Christ Jesus on behalf of you Gentiles" (v. 1).

The Revelation of God's Secret to Paul (3:2-6)

In verse 1, Paul probably intended to begin a prayer. Then in verse 2, he departed abruptly from his thought in order to comment on his role as a minister to the Gentiles. Finally, in verse 14, he returned to his prayer.

Paul's statement in verse 2 seems to indicate that he did not know at least some of his intended readers personally, for he assumed that they had heard of his role in God's plan. Since Paul had labored at Ephesus for about three years, the Ephesians would have come to know him well. If he had been writing to those people, he would not have made an assumption about their acquaintance with his ministry. Also, he would not have felt the necessity of explaining his role in missions to the Gentiles.

Paul described his function in God's redemptive plan as a "stewardship" of God's grace. (v. 2). As noted previously, "stewardship" (*oikonomia*) has two basic meanings. The word can refer to a plan or an arrangement. Or, it can refer to the steward's responsibility. Here, the latter meaning fits in the context better. Paul probably had in mind his own responsibility which God had given to him.

What did Paul mean when he wrote "of the stewardship of God's grace that was given to me" (v. 2)? One possibility is that Paul thought of his task as administering God's grace to Gentiles. This interpretation poses some problems. One problem arises from the grammar of the text, where the participle "given" modifies "grace" rather than "stewardship." Probably we should understand that Paul saw his role—apostle to the Gentiles—as one which was due solely to God's grace. He was not worthy of the task to which God had called him. Unworthy though he was, Paul knew that God had given him this grace—this unmerited favor—of performing a crucial role in opening the way for Gentiles into God's new community. He was given the opportunity of preaching to them the good news.

How did Paul know about God's plan? He wrote that it was "by revelation" (v. 3). "Revelation" simply underlined the fact that God was the source of Paul's insight.

Paul did not describe the means of revelation or his experience when he received it. He believed that God, through his Spirit, was active in the world and that he was able to communicate with his people. (See 1 Cor. 14:6,26.) From this point of view, revelation never ceases. We believe that God revealed himself in a unique series of events, culminating in his revelation through Jesus Christ. He continues to reveal himself to people through his Spirit.

Paul classified his particular revelation from God, and God's similar disclosure to others, in a special category. God's revelation to Paul disclosed a key element in God's eternal plan of redemption. This disclosure to Paul was not just any revelation; it was a crucial revelation. God had revealed to Paul "the mystery," or even better, the secret. Previously, the secret had been unknown. But God had not meant for Paul to keep the revelation a secret. He was to publish God's secret in the widest possible manner.

"As I have written briefly" (v. 3) could refer to a letter that Paul had written previously. But more likely, it points to what Paul already had written about the secret in Ephesians (1:7-10).

Paul defined the secret as the "secret of Christ" [the Messiah] (v. 4). Paul understood that the Messiah's function in creating a new humanity constituted the revelation that God gave him.

Paul mentioned two groups of people as recipients of God's new revelation. Paul certainly would agree that God had revealed himself to the prophets of the Old Testament. He undoubtedly would agree that certain writings were God's revelation to people. He quoted some passages from the Old Testament in Ephesians.

This secret or "mystery" was the element that had not been known before (v. 5). People knew that God was active. They had received and delivered God's word to their generations. But they had not been aware of what God was up to in all his activity. They really had not understood where God's activity was leading.

But in his own time, God had given this insight into his secret "to his holy apostles and prophets by the Spirit" (v. 5). The apostles were a special group of people with a unique function in God's redemptive purpose. They were the ones to whom the risen Lord had appeared and to whom he had given a commission. Paul considered himself to be one of this group.

The apostles were witnesses to Jesus' life, death, and resurrection. They performed the function for the early Christians that the New Testament, the apostolic witness, performs for us today. But what Paul wrote about in Ephesians went beyond that. To be a living witness to the death and resurrection of Jesus was one thing. To understand the meaning of the event was another. This understanding of the Christ event was the secret that God had made known to the apostles. Galatians 2:9 corroborates the fact that apostles other than Paul had understood the scope of God's redemptive plan. According to Paul's own testimony, James, Cephas (Peter), and John shared his understanding of the gospel.

Paul called this group "holy apostles" (v. 5). This phrase has a different ring for us than it did for Paul. To us, "holy" means especially good or saintly. But Paul used the word in the biblical sense of that which belongs to God. Anything is holy which has been set apart for God's service. To Paul, all Christians were holy. One of his favorite terms for all believers was the word that we translate "saints" in verses such as Romans 1:7, 15:26; 1 Corinthians 1:2; Ephesians 1:1. The saints might have been bad, good, or mediocre. But they were all saints because they were God's people.

Thus, to call the apostles holy did not necessarily set them apart from other Christians. The term did distinguish the apostles from messengers or emissaries of the secular world. The apostles were God's agents, commissioned to deliver his message.

The "prophets" mentioned by Paul no doubt were New Testament prophets. One of the basic New Testament teachings is that with the saving event of Jesus Christ, the Spirit was given to the church. One of the

Spirit's gifts was the gift of prophecy.

Prophecy was simply the proclamation of God's word to his people. Unfortunately, today the English word *prophecy* has the connotation of prediction. This is the meaning we often read into the biblical passage. However, prophecy can deal with present, past, or future; it is the proclamation of the message that a person receives from God, whatever that message may be.

In verse 6, Paul stated the content of this prophetic message. God had revealed that Gentiles were to be included in Israel, the redeemed community, on the same basis as Jews. The Gentiles were not to be second-class citizens in the covenant community. The policy Israel had followed in dealing with Gentiles was not to be the pattern for the church. Terms like foreigner, sojourner, and proselyte no longer were to be used.

English translations have difficulty in preserving Paul's emphasis on the equality of Gentiles with Jews in sharing God's blessings. In verse 6, each word describing the Gentiles' new status in the church has a prefix which means with. These words might be translated coheirs, comembers of the body, copartakers of the promise.

In Paul's description of the Gentiles' new status, he began with the future and moved to the past. In the future, Gentiles will share without prejudice in all the blessings of eternity. They are coheirs. God will make no distinction among his children. At the moment, the Gentiles were members of the body—the church—just as much as any believing Jew was. They were members "of the *same* body" (v. 6). They also shared as beneficiaries in God's promises on the same level as the Jews. They were copartakers "of the promise."

In verse 6, the promises were all included in the one promise. The one promise was God's promise realized in the Messiah, Jesus. The inclusion of the Gentiles took place through the gospel. When the gospel was proclaimed to Gentiles and they responded to it, people once excluded became members of God's people without any vestige of prejudice or liability.

The Revelation of God's Secret Through Paul (3:7-13)

Paul had been made a "minister" of the gospel for all people (v. 7). The word "minister" translates the Greek term which means servant and describes the function of waiting on tables.

Paul's relationship to the gospel, therefore, was put in its right perspective. His calling was to serve the gospel. This sense of calling is contrary to the tendency observed so often today in which people use the gospel to further their own ends. The servant of the gospel does not exploit it for power or profit. His life is ordered by it and finds its meaning in the service it demands. The gospel was meant for all people, and Paul served it when he proclaimed it to the Gentiles.

Paul further defined his ministry as "the gift of God's grace" (v. 7). This truth was emphasized by the use of the redundant modifying phrase. It was a gift of the "grace" of God. "Grace" is God's undeserved love that comes to us without regard to our own accomplishments or worthiness. Anything that is an expression of God's grace comes to us as a gift.

Paul went on to define his ministry with the phrase "by the working of his [God's] power" (v. 7). This phrase brings out the idea that Paul did not accomplish anything through his own strength. If in his proclamation of the gospel people had been converted, lives had been changed, churches had been created, these were to be explained in terms of God's power. Paul took no credit at all for the accomplishments of his ministry.

In order to make even more emphatic the incredible wonder of God's grace, Paul went on to describe himself as "the very least of all the saints" (v. 8). As noted previously, "saints" in this phrase included all God's people. What Paul meant was that of all Christians, he was the most unlikely candidate for the role to which God had called him. No doubt, Paul's reason for saying this was his memory of his former hostility toward the gospel. He had led in the persecution of the church. He had hated the name of Jesus with a deep and raging passion. Because of Paul, Jesus' followers had suffered. He had perceived that the gospel threatened Jewish exclusiveness. He had been fanatically devoted to that exclusiveness. Thus, he had become an uncompromising enemy of the church.

We can understand what Paul meant by grace only when we remember his background. For Paul, "grace" meant completely undeserved love. He had been a thoroughgoing rebel against God when God had saved him and called him. He could not attribute his salvation to any personal merit. He had not been seeking to be saved; he had not been weeping at a mourner's bench; and he had not been praying for God to change his life. The only way he could explain God's action on his behalf was in terms of grace.

As Paul wrote about his ministry, he divided it into two parts. One of his responsibilities was "to preach to the Gentiles the unsearchable riches of Christ" (v. 8). Paul thought of himself as the apostle to the Gentiles. God had given to him the task of the pioneer. Formerly the Pharisee of the Pharisees, he had been singled out to break down the wall that people like him had erected to separate Jew from Gentile. He had been called to convey the message of God's saving power to those people whom formerly he had thought to be outside the realm of God's redemptive plan.

The paradox faced by the preacher is conveyed, perhaps unconsciously, by Paul's phrase "to preach . . . the unsearchable riches of Christ." "Unsearchable" describes that which is beyond human power to comprehend and human tongue to articulate. So Paul admitted that the task to which he had been called was beyond his ability to accomplish. In a real sense, those who preach the gospel are called to do something at which they are destined to be failures from the outset. Mind cannot comprehend, nor can words describe what Christ means to the person who turns to him in faith.

Arrogance is a sin of which many preachers are also guilty. Some egotistical preachers are proud because they believe they are more articulate than others. Or, perhaps, their statistics are better. But humility is the sincere preacher's only appropriate stance. When he compares what he has said to the reality he is trying to present, he always is aware that he has failed miserably. Only the power of God can take the words of preachers and make them effective, productive.

Paul described the second aspect of his ministry in verse 9: "to make all men see what is the plan of the mystery."

The word translated "plan" in the Revised Standard Version is the Greek word *oikonomia*. As we have noted previously, this is one of the two major possibilities in understanding the term. The context seems to demand this choice of meanings at this point, rather than "stewardship" as it was translated in 3:2.

Paul wanted to help people understand this wonderful plan of redemption put into effect through Jesus, the Messiah—a plan so vast in its scope that it could include both Gentiles and Jews. Paul not only felt a responsibility for preaching to the Gentiles. He also was called to help Jews understand that God had included Gentiles. On the other hand, he wanted Gentiles to understand the place of Jews in God's redemption. (See Rom. 11.) This understanding was essential for Jews and Gentiles if they were to accept each other as fellow members of Christ's body.

God's secret had been "hidden for ages" (v. 9). Paul recognized that the previous generations had failed to perceive God's intention to bring Gentiles and Jews together in the Messiah. Some people call this concept progressive revelation. This term, however, may convey an erroneous connotation. If we mean by progressive revelation that humanity has increased its capacity to understand God's words and ways, that idea was foreign to Paul. If we mean, however, that God has unfolded his purpose step by step to his people, then we are close to Paul's concept of revelation. God's action, and not man's progress, was determinative for Paul.

But Paul believed that what God was doing had a significance beyond the human scene. "Through the church the manifold wisdom of God" was being made known "to the principalities and powers in the heavenly places" (v. 10). The miracle that brought the church into being had a cosmic effect. When Paul referred to "principalities and powers," he probably had in mind the hostile spiritual powers from which Christians had been delivered by the gospel. They were the powers that opposed the work of God. They were the enemies of God who were trying to fragment his universe. Paul believed that these powers could see how futile their efforts were to frustrate God's purpose.

God's demonstration of wisdom before the powers was made "through the church" (v. 10). The church is the evidence of God's many-faceted "wisdom." This is indeed an amazing idea. When people have sought proof for God's existence, they often have turned to nature. When they have sought to extol his wisdom, they frequently have pointed to the intricacies of natural law. But Paul believed that one must look at the church in order to see how wonderful God's ways are.

The church—where diverse, hostile, uncongenial people have been brought together in a family of love—is the greatest demonstration of the hostile forces' failure. Here the prejudice that has poisoned people's hearts has been dealt with. Here the walls of race, class, and culture that have isolated people from one another have been brought down. Perhaps in the light of this concept of the church, we can begin to understand why relationships in the church were so important to Paul. A church divided by the prejudices and hostilities of the world is a contradiction. Where such divided churches exist, the evil powers can point to them and mock God.

But where grace and love have brought people together, the sign of God's future is evident. The evidence is given that he can fulfill his purpose. The powerful forces have been defeated that have brought epidemics, murder, war, famine, and loneliness to the world.

So the church is exhibit A in God's showcase. Even in the churches in Paul's day, this concept often was more of a promise than a reality. But this promise furnished the demand under which the church lived; it was a standard by which God's people could measure their life together as the church. And in some cases, as in Paul's own experience, the promise had been actualized.

Once again, in verse 11, we are reminded that God's working through his church is not a makeshift emergency arrangement. God's redemptive use of the church was in accord with his "eternal purpose." Once again, we are reminded of Jesus the Messiah's centrality in this redemptive plan. Through Christ Jesus, God has realized his purpose.

Paul wrote first about the new relationship of believers to one another. After this, in verse 12, he began to describe their new relationship with God. This was his order once before in 2:13-22. This order should remind us of how wrong and perverted some contemporary concepts of the gospel are. Some people decry involvement in social concerns. They say that their only important concern is to get people right with God. But Paul knew that people who were not right with one another could not be right with God.

Through Jesus Christ, Gentiles and Jews had been brought together in a new fellowship with one another. Also, through him they had new possibilities in their relationship to God.

This new stance toward God was characterized first by "boldness" (v. 12). The believers no longer were terrified and unsure of themselves before God. The word translated "boldness" has to do primarily with boldness in speech. Paul may have been thinking about prayer when he used this word. Believers can talk to God without fear; they can lay before him whatever concerns or troubles them. They do not have to be afraid that God will get them if they say something out of place or in the wrong way.

The object of ritual in religion is to set up patterns by which people can approach God or the gods without fear of doing it wrong. For people who are in terror of God, the approach to him literally is a mine field heavily sowed with taboos.

Sometimes people ask me: "Is it all right to pray about this, or in this way?" My answer is: "God's child can say anything to God that he or she wants to say." We can talk to him without fear because we know that he is not against us. He is for us. That we should think about and discuss the theology of prayer is inescapable. However, the child of God who talks to him in loving confidence, trusting in his goodness and power, is always closer to the truth than is the theologian.

Once again, as in 2:18, Paul affirmed that no hindrances blocked the believer's worship of God. We have "confidence of access through our faith" in Christ (v. 12).

Thus, in this passage we have Paul's view of the church. The church is a community without walls. No walls separate the believer from brothers and sisters in Christ. No walls separate the believer from God.

The last phrase of verse 12 is ambiguous, and this ambiguity is reflected in the translations. The King James Version translates "by the faith of him." The Revised Standard Version reads "through our faith in him." Grammatically and theologically, both are possible. Grammatically, the King James Version's is the most natural one. If it is correct, Paul meant that our new life before God is the result of Christ's faithfulness. Obviously, this is a true affirmation, and it fits well into Paul's theology.

If the Revised Standard Version is correct, Paul meant that as believers in Jesus Christ we have access to God. This is probably the correct interpretation, for it seems to fit the immediate context better. Through Jesus Christ, our way to God is opened. Our faith in him is nothing more or less than our decision to walk in the way he has opened up.

In the light of all that Paul had written, his readers were to evaluate his sufferings or tribulations. (See the King James Version for a literal translation of v. 13.) The noun "sufferings" in the original text is an interesting and important word in the New Testament. It does not denote just any suffering or trial. It refers specifically to those that the believer experiences *as a believer*. In an evil and hostile world, the faithful believer's inescapable lot is to suffer as a result of his or her loyalty to Christ.

But Paul believed his suffering to be an inescapable part of God's unfolding redemptive plan. The only way Gentiles could receive the gospel was for Paul to challenge the world's power structures that opposed God's plan. That he would pay the price for that challenge was inevitable. Paul wrote in more detail about his sufferings for the gospel in 2 Corinthians 11:23-27. Paul's sufferings, therefore, were the Gentiles' "glory" (v. 13). To understand precisely how Paul used the term "glory" is difficult. Most often, he referred to the believer's future glory—his eternal life in God's presence. Perhaps Paul meant to say that his suffering was bound up with his readers' salvation in such a way that his suffering became a part of their redemption. His suffering was essential if they were to be heirs of God's future; Gentiles could not be saved if people like Paul were not willing to suffer.

Whatever the precise meaning of the word "glory," the idea is clear. Paul's readers were not to view Paul's imprisonment as a defeat, shame, or humiliation. These are always believers' possible reactions to trial. Believers can become dispirited and defeated, thinking that their cause is lost.

The Reason for Preaching the Gospel

A popular contemporary religion has revived the old erroneous notion that wealth, health, and success are evidences of God's power and presence. I recently heard a testimony by a successful businessman on one of the more popular religious television shows. According to his testimony, he had wandered away from God and had allowed sin to come into his life. Things went from bad to worse in his personal and business life. But he turned around in his spiritual life and made a new commitment of himself to Christ. Now everything was rosy and his business was booming.

A person might use this slogan: Believe in Jesus and get rich. Or: Believe in Jesus and stay healthy. These ideas, expressed or unexpressed, run through much of religion today.

Needless to say, we are in a different atmosphere as we read Ephesians 3:1-13. For Paul, just the opposite was true. Tribulation, not success and wealth, was the sign of God's presence, the evidence that his purpose was moving along. Just as Paul applied the Old Testament passage in Romans, we, too, may say: " 'For thy sake we are being killed all the day long' " (Rom. 8:36). Suffering and not good fortune may be the prelude to glory.

Paul did not preach the gospel to the Gentiles for personal gain. As we know, he had to pay a terrible price to do it. He pursued his ministry because he believed that it was in keeping with what God was doing. He preached the gospel because he believed it was true, not because he believed it would work in the world's sense of the term.

Personal Learning Activities

1. According to Dr. Tolbert, Paul probably wrote Ephesians while imprisoned in (choose the correct answer from the following list):
   _____(1) Jerusalem
   _____(2) Caesarea
   _____(3) Ephesus
   _____(4) Rome

2. Match the two lists, linking term with definition:
   _____(1) Stewardship   (a) Servant who waits on tables
   _____(2) Revelation   (b) The coming of the Messiah
   _____(3) Apostles   (c) Proclaimers of God's word to his people
   _____(4) Prophets   (d) Responsibility given by God
   _____(5) God's promise (e) God's gift of insight
   _____(6) Minister   (f) Witnesses of Jesus' life, death, and
                               resurrection

3. According to Paul, what was God's mystery or open secret?

4. The _____ is the greatest demonstration of the failure of
   hostile forces in our universe. (Choose the proper response from the
   list.)
   (1) Home
   (2) Church
   (3) Nation
   (4) State

5. God has realized his redemptive purpose through the apostles,
   prophets, and deacons. True _____ False _____

6. According to Dr. Tolbert, God's child can say anything in prayer that he
   or she wants to say. True _____ False _____

7. Paul wanted his readers to view his imprisonment as (select the correct
   answer from the list):
   _____(1) Defeat
   _____(2) Shame
   _____(3) Humiliation
   _____(4) Glory

Answers:
1. (4); 2. (1)d, (2)e, (3)f, (4)c, (5)b, (6)a; 3. The Gentiles are to be included in the people of God on an equal basis with believing Jews.
4. (2); 5. False; 6. True; 7. (4).

6

Paul's Prayer for the Saints

Ephesians 3:14-21

Evidently, in Ephesians 3:1, Paul intended to begin the prayer that we find in 3:14-21. In 3:2, he interrupted his thought with his remarks about his ministry to the Gentiles. In 3:14, as he went back to his line of thought, he repeated the opening phrase of 3:1 and proceeded to share with his readers his petitions to God on their behalf.

Prayer to the Father (3:14-15)

What is presupposed by the phrase "for this reason" (v. 14) is not clear. Perhaps all that Paul had written in the first two chapters is what motivated him to pray for the believers. Because of what God had done for them, he could ask God to bless them and could be confident that his prayer would be heard. They were members of God's household. God was their Father. Because they were his own, God willed to complete in these Gentile believers that marvelous work which he had begun in their lives.

Perhaps Paul thought more specifically about his idea expressed in 2:18. Since believers have access to God through the Spirit, Paul was confident that he could go to God on behalf of his readers. Prayer became a possibility and a responsibility because of what God had done for his children.

The Arcadian Way in Ephesus leading out toward the harbor

At any rate, Paul believed that he could and should pray for other Christians. Contemporary Christians raise all kinds of theological questions about prayer. Does prayer change God? Why pray at all? God loves his people more than we do; will he not act in love toward them apart from our prayers? These are typical questions.

Whatever our answers to those questions, Paul believed that part of his responsibility toward other believers was to pray for them. He evidently felt that his praying would make a difference. He must have believed that intercession for others was part of God's pattern for his church.

Whatever Paul meant by "for this reason" (v. 1), he believed that prayer for believers was possible, essential, and worthwhile. If our theology of prayer does not support this conclusion, we probably need to reexamine it. Belief in the importance of prayer for others certainly is supported by the New Testament and by Christian experience.

Paul described his posture in prayer: "I bow my knees" (v. 14). This was not the usual posture for prayer in the Old Testament or in the Jewish community contemporary with Paul. The Old Testament gives us only a few examples of prayers uttered by people on their knees. Jews generally stood when they prayed. To kneel or prostrate oneself before God was a sign of crisis or of intensity in prayer.

Kneeling or prostrating oneself before God in prayer may have been more common in the Gentile churches. In the Gentiles' society, to do obeisance before kings and deities in this manner was common. This may have influenced the form of Gentile worship.

Paul addressed his petition to the "Father" (v. 14). The word for Father here is *patera*. Jesus used the word *abba* when he addressed God and taught his disciples to use the term. In the context of Jesus' teaching, *abba* was an intimate term. *Abba* (father) was one of the first words Hebrew children learned to say. It was the word used by little children in speaking to their fathers. For Jesus, the relationship of a good earthly father to his little children was an analogy of the relationship between God and his children. God loves and cares for his children. They can trust completely and implicitly in his care. This childlike attitude of trust and dependence frees them from anxiety about the future.

Christian prayer, as taught by Jesus, presupposes all that is contained in the word "Father." We can talk to God without fear, and we can trust him to respond in love.

This concept of God as a loving, trustworthy Father could be involved also in Paul's use of the term *patera*. As a believer, following Jesus' pattern and teaching, he went to God in prayer as one going to his Father.

But the context shows that Paul also had another implication in mind that was important to the context of Ephesians. God is the "Father, from whom every family in heaven and on earth is named" (vv. 14-15). This qualifying statement is difficult, as the varying translations indicate.

A textual problem exists. Some manuscripts read "the Father of our Lord Jesus Christ" (KJV). But the evidence supports the shorter reading of the Revised Standard Version. Be that as it may, we may rest assured that for Paul, the concept of God as Father arose out of his faith in Jesus.

Some interpreters hold that Paul thought of God's being the Father of believers as the archetype of all other fatherhood. This idea asserts that the concept of father, wherever it exists, derives its reality and its meaning from the fatherhood of God. The source of the father relationship ultimately is God. This concept of archetypical relationships is more platonic than Semitic, however, and probably was not decisive in Paul's thinking.

What was the idea conveyed by Paul's statement? We probably are not far off base if we conclude that Paul had two emphases in mind. He thought about the universality of the fatherhood of God, and he also stressed the ascendancy or sovereignty of God as Father. God is the universal Father in the sense that he is the Creator of people, the Source of life. He is Father in a unique, special sense to those who have responded to him in faith. He brings responsive people into his family and becomes the Father who nurtures. He is the sovereign Lord who is, at heart, most like a Father—in the best sense of the term.

When Paul wrote of families in heaven and on earth (v. 15), he probably did not have in mind concepts or ideas. For him, families were realities. For the Hebrew, the term "family" was a concrete one. It denoted specific families that derived their existence from common fathers who were their heads. The word translated "family" (*patria*) also was used in an extended way to refer to clans and nations.

When Paul spoke of heavenly families, he did not employ an unusual Jewish expression. For example, Jewish literature contains references to families of angels. God, therefore, is the cosmic Father. As Creator, his fatherhood embraces all peoples and powers. God's universal fatherhood in the sense of redemptive grace finds its expression in the church, where people from different nations and tribes call him Father and are, in fact, his children.

The text reads that the families on earth and in heaven receive their names from God (v. 15). The business of naming the children belonged to the father. This right expressed the authority he had over the children whom he named. In Genesis 2:20, for example, Adam's authority over other creatures is expressed in his naming them.

God is called Father of every group, however designated, because he is the reason for the groups' existence. He brought everything into existence by his creative power. His position is expressed by his fatherly act of begetting his children. Therefore, Paul emphasized the exalted position of God with reference to all other beings, whether earthly or celestial. God preceded them as Creator; he is superior to them as Father. God's redemptive purpose includes all; his purpose is cosmic in its reach, as we have seen already.

Believers recognize that God is the Father of all in the sense that he created all. His fatherhood has significance even when people reject it or rebel against it. People's rebellion does not diminish God's position and cannot frustrate his purpose.

The Requests in Paul's Prayer (3:16-19)

To isolate the individual requests in Paul's prayer and to see their exact inner relationships as well as their distinctiveness is difficult. From most versions, one would think that the prayer contained four or more distinct requests. If we allow the Greek syntax to determine our understanding of the prayer's structure, we will see three major requests in it. They are: (1) a petition for inner strengthening (vv. 16-17), (2) a prayer for comprehension of Christ's love (vv. 18-19a), and (3) a request for complete filling (v. 19b).

Prayer for Inner Strengthening

The first request Paul made to God on behalf of his readers was that they might be "strengthened with might" (v. 16). Paul used some of the same terminology in Ephesians 1:9 in a previous prayer for them. There the emphasis was different. Paul wanted believers to be aware of the extent of God's marvelous power which he had exercised in their behalf.

The apostle was concerned about the strength of the believer to become what God intended that person to be. This strength is not something that arises from the Christian's own personal capacity. It is a gift from God. The Christian only has the strength that he or she receives.

The believer's life is determined by God's grace from beginning to end. Each unbeliever was saved by grace, and he or she lives by grace. Each one was redeemed by God's power and is sustained by his power.

Once again, Paul emphasized the limitless resources which God has. God strengthens his children "according to the riches of his glory" (v. 16). The well from which we draw our strength has no bottom because its measure is God's own glory. "Glory" in this text stands for all that God is and has; it is his infinite majesty and power.

Believers are strengthened "through his [God's] Spirit" (v. 16). "Spirit" is the Holy Spirit, present and active in the lives of believers. Through God's gift of his Spirit to us, we are not condemned to struggle alone in our adversities and temptations. God is present to empower and help us.

In its translation of the last phrase of verse 16, the Revised Standard

Version reads "in the inner man." In the Greek text, however, the preposition is different, and we can translate: unto (*eis*) the inner man. If it retains its original force in this passage, the preposition denotes motion toward. In this case, "the inner man" denotes the goal toward which the believer moves and for which he or she needs strength. The center of the new life, therefore, has been transformed by God's redeeming power.

What the child of God needs is strength to make his or her total life coherent with that person's new existence as a member of God's family. The contradiction between our attitudes and acts and our profession of faith needs to be removed. Only God's power can do this.

If we allow the Greek syntax to determine our interpretation, verse 17 will be a parallel statement to the one made in verse 16. What does it mean to be strengthened unto the inner man? Another way of expressing it is that Christ dwells in our hearts. The verb translated "may dwell" (RSV) literally is to dwell, (an infinitive in the Greek text). It is a cognate of the noun translated "dwelling place" in Ephesians 2:22.

According to Paul's theology, the real temple is God's people—the church—or the individual's heart. Elements are present for a Trinitarian theology in Ephesians. But whatever Paul's concept of the Trinity may have been, he did not incline at all toward polytheism. He could refer to God's presence in the believers' lives on one occasion, the Spirit's presence on another, and in verse 17 to Christ's presence. The oneness of Father, Son, and Spirit were such that no distinction was made in their presence or activity in believers' lives. If our doctrine of the Trinity is to be truly New Testament, we must preserve this monotheistic emphasis.

Our hearts become temples for the living Lord "through faith" (v. 17). This means that our acceptance of Christ and our openness to him always are met by the response of his presence. No program of works or human merit exists that can guarantee his presence in our lives. Only when we recognize our need and our helplessness and trust in him does he come to us to supply our need.

In the Revised Standard Version, "rooted and grounded in love" is connected with the statement in verse 18. This connection is possible, but in the light of the Greek grammar, I prefer to place it with verses 16 and 17.

Paul was fond of joining faith and love which he seems to have done at this point. What is the life of faith? It is a life rooted and grounded in love. Here Paul mixed his metaphors. The first, "rooted," is an agricultural figure; and the second, "grounded," is an analogy from construction. The roots of a plant must go deep into rich soil if the plant is to experience proper growth. The builders of a temple must be concerned first about its foundation if their work is to have an enduring quality.

"Love" is the soil in which the believer is rooted and the foundation on which the Christian's life is built. Of course, the love Paul had in mind was

not just any love. This love is God's love expressed in his self-giving
through Christ. Moreover, God's love is active in the believing community
and is expressed in the relationship among Christians.

What Paul was concerned about in his request was growth toward
Christian maturity. Always, he conceived this in terms of faith and love
that stand at the beginning, in the middle, and at the consummation of the
Christian life.

Prayer for Knowledge of Christ's Love

Second, Paul requested for his readers the "power" (or, perhaps better,
strength) to comprehend something (v. 18). Once again, we note that even
the ability to perceive God's truth does not arise from within. Such ability
is given by God himself.

Some people tend to be arrogant because they judge their knowledge of
the Bible to be superior to the ordinary Christian's. They know the original languages. What mystery is contained in that assertion! They can
quote the German, English, and American theologians—people who are
strangers to most church members. They can bulwark their interpretations with copious footnotes.

But what Paul was concerned that believers comprehend was not to be
obtained by a knowledge of languages, facts, or the latest theological
trends. What he was concerned about did not depend on IQ or on studying
at the best schools. What Paul wished his readers to comprehend was not a
puzzle to be unlocked by tenacious mental effort. It was a gift to be
bestowed by God on those characterized by humble receptiveness rather
than arrogant self-confidence.

Paul wanted his readers to comprehend something that was overwhelm-
ing in its vastness. From where the believer stood, it extended to either
side of him in incredible breadth; it stretched out in front of him to infinite
distances; it reached above him to dizzying heights; and it plunged be-
neath him to awesome depths.

Whatever Paul had in mind, it was to be comprehended "with all the
saints" (v. 18). The gift of an awareness, an insight, was to be received in
fellowship with other believers. This stress on fellowship is a consistent
emphasis in Ephesians. God's truth is not a private truth. His revelation is
not an esoteric revelation. The redemption he has provided is not the
personal property of any individual. Only in the fellowship of the church is
revealed the fullness of his truth.

We do well to look with suspicion on people who claim to know things
that other believers do not know, who claim to have received a unique
revelation that has been denied to others.

In speaking to Christian groups, I often stress that the important things
I say are those they already know. I may know something about the

language of the New Testament or the culture of the Hellenistic world that
most church members do not know. But these matters are peripheral.
God's important truths are available to all his people. Or, to say it another
way: If my grandmother did not know it, it is not too important. She was
the best Christian I knew in my childhood. She knew the things that are
essential to the Christian life far better than I or many of my highly
educated contemporaries.

But a question remains. What is this thing—so wide, so long, so high, so
deep—that Paul wished the believers to comprehend? He did not say.
Many suggestions have been made concerning what Paul had in view. The
best conclusion seems to be that Paul thought about "the love of Christ"
that he mentioned in verse 19.

How do we know Christ's love, so vast in its dimensions? The answer is
simple, yet difficult. We know it in our experiences of being loved by him.
Christ's love becomes clearer in our awareness of the depths from which
we have been lifted or the heights to which we have been transported. We
comprehend it as we open our lives to Christ's love and become a channel
to transmit it to others. This love becomes defined more sharply as we
begin to ignore the differences, the disadvantages, the faults, the dirt, the
disease of others and start loving them without reservation. We know
Christ's love as we open our arms and hearts to all our brothers and sisters;
as we accept them, whatever their background, race, condition, or station
in life; and as we rejoice in their fellowship.

Paul's request contained an inevitable contradiction. He wanted God to
help believers know something "which surpasses knowledge" (v. 19). This
contradiction presents us with the tension that is both our despair and our
challenge, our judgment and our hope.

No matter where we are in our comprehension of Christ's love, it towers
above us and stretches out before us. This is our despair. But our challenge
lies in the opportunity to continue the pilgrimage in the exhilaration of
prospective new discoveries to be made in the future.

Our judgment is that our knowledge of Christ's love always is limited by
our prejudice and selfishness. But love's vastness also is our hope. Christ
loves us when we do not deserve to be loved. He loves us more than we love
him or others. Because of his loving us, we can endure the tension.

Prayer for Complete Filling
Finally, Paul prayed that his readers might "be filled with all the fulness
of God" (v. 19). All these petitions underline one truth: Paul, although
probably unacquainted personally with his readers, knew that they had
not reached the acme of the Christian experience or life.

One thing becomes clear from Paul's letters: the members of those early
churches often were imperfect, weak, erring, sinful—just as believers are

Diana (Artemis) of the Ephesians

today. Thus, the possibility always existed for more of God to be in the believer's life as long as he or she lived in the world. This was axiomatic for the apostle. The reason for the possibility of having more of God in a life is that God always has more to give than the believer has received. A distance always lies between the believer and the goal to which God is moving him or her.

The preposition "with" in the Revised Standard Version's translation of the phrase is possible. In fact, most of the translations agree with it. However, "with" is not the literal translation of the Greek *eis* which denotes motion toward someone or something. This preposition possibly should retain its earlier force in the text. If so, we would translate it: unto the fullness of God (v. 19). Paul had this incredible view of the possibility of the Christian's life: We can be filled to the fullness of God. That is, we never should be satisfied until we have received all that God has to give.

One caution is in order. Paul was no mystic in the sense of believing that the individual eventually merged into God and thereby lost his or her own identity. A distinction always exists between the believer and God. This distinction is preserved because the believer never loses his or her status as the recipient, and God is always the giver.

Probably the three petitions we have discussed should be understood as practical equivalents. To be strengthened unto the inner man, to know in experience Christ's love, and to be filled with God's fullness are all one and the same thing.

The Closing Doxology (3:20-21)

As we read Paul's prayer, we are struck by its splendor. Some people consider this to be the outstanding passage in the whole epistle. Inspired by the limitless possibilities of the Christian life as measured only by God's capacity to give, Paul soared into the heights as he envisioned his readers' future.

Paul's reaction was significant. He was impressed by his limitations in prayer and his ability to conceive of the possibilities inherent in God's grace. His poor and meager capacity could not express in words that which was worthy and adequate.

But Paul's inability did not induce despair, for he believed in prayer—in its necessity and its efficacy. He believed that intercessory prayer was important. But he believed also in God's freedom to act according to his own love and power.

The fact that our prayers are limited both in their conception and articulation does not limit God. He is not governed by the limits our ignorance and sin impose on us.

Therefore, Paul praised God as the one who can and will do "far more abundantly than all that we ask or think" (v. 20). Our prayer does not determine the extent of God's blessings on us. Rather, his "power at work within us" (v. 20) is the measure of our life's possibilities as his children.

What should be our response to the great, loving, and giving God? Paul thought God deserved "glory in the church and in Christ Jesus" (v. 21). This phrase is puzzling and difficult. The questions raised are twofold. Why did Paul refer to the church and Christ (the Messiah) in parallel phrases that distinguish between them and make them, at least in this text, equivalent? Second, why did he put the church before the Messiah, Jesus?

The difficulty was seen early, a fact we detect from the variety of readings in the manuscripts. Some manuscripts omit the conjunction "and" so that the reading is: in the church in Christ Jesus. This accords with an idea characteristic of Ephesians. All the believers' activity is in or through Christ Jesus. Some early versions and some of the church fathers reverse the order of the phrases. They read: in Christ Jesus and in the church. The weight of the evidence, however, is on the side of the reading chosen by the Revised Standard Version's translators.

Modern interpreters may—and probably do—make too much of such nuances. What Paul believed is beyond doubt: (1) Jesus Christ was the reason for the existence of the church; (2) the church's relationship to God in every sphere was in and through Jesus Christ; (3) the church praised and worshiped God in and through Christ; and (4) Christ glorified God supremely.

Now we ask: What does it mean to say "to him be glory in the church" (v. 21)?

What is intended includes the church's worship of God. Someone has said that the church's distinctive characteristic is its worship of God. Many groups gather for many purposes. The church assembles, however, to worship God. But more is involved than public worship, for the church's worship can be a scandal if there is too much contradiction between what it says, and what it is and does.

The church glorifies God when it manifests its character as God's redeemed people to the world. When the church shows that the power of God has overcome the power of sin, it glorifies God. When God's people show that God's Spirit has bound them together in a loving family that disregards the world's categories, they glorify God.

Paul was convinced that praise to God has two sources: the church and the Christ. But these are not to be thought of as separate and distinct, if we respect the theology of Ephesians. Glory to God in the church is possible because Christ has glorified God. So the two sources, rightly seen, constitute one source from which glory is ascribed to God.

Praise of God is to be the characteristic of the church and her Messiah through all the aeons that stretch ahead. Paul stressed the unending duration of our praise to God by the redundant phrases at the end of chapter 3. "To all generations" is the same as "for ever and ever" (v. 21). Apparently, some professing Christians will have to change a lot if they are to enjoy heaven. They do not enjoy praising God for one hour each week; they think worship is dull and boring, a lot less interesting than golf or something else. How are they going to enjoy worship that never ends?

The Truth for Life

The Christian life is exciting because it is not static. Always, new possibilities beckon us from ahead. Whatever we have known, experienced, or received is only an indication of something better, greater, and higher that awaits us in our Christian pilgrimage. God still has a great deal to do in all our lives. He has a lot to show us and much to give us.

A disturbing tendency keeps cropping up among Christians. It is the tendency to regard some great experience or revelation from God as the norm for the Christian life. When a person has reached this high level of complete surrender or complete filling, that individual may feel that he or she has arrived. The counterpart of this is arrogance. A person may be tempted to look down on others who have not had his or her experience. The efforts of such an individual then are directed toward trying to help other people have the same level of experience. Any experience is misunderstood if it is seen as the ultimate, the final, or the highest possible one. Any experience, however glorious, and any insight, however penetrating, are interpreted properly only if they are seen as the necessary step before we can take the next one.

To pray as Paul did is always appropriate. To ask that we and our brothers and sisters be strengthened so that we can know the love of Christ and so that God can fill us always is in order.

We are never as strong as we can be; we never know Christ's love in all its dimensions; and we never have all that God can give us.

Personal Learning Activities

1. In Ephesians 3:14, Paul addressed God as _____ in his prayer.
   (Choose the proper response from the list.)
   (1) Lord

    (2) Creator

    (3) Father

2. _____ is the soil in which the believer is rooted and the foundation on which the Christian's life is built. (Select the correct answer.)

    (1) Wisdom

    (2) Worship

    (3) Love

    (4) Humility

3. The stress on fellowship is a rather minor emphasis in Ephesians. True _____ False _____

4. The incredible possibility of the Christian life, for Paul, is that the Christian (choose the correct response from the list):

    _____ (1) Can be filled with the fullness of God

    _____ (2) Can achieve sinless perfection

    _____ (3) Can be free of trouble

5. Our prayers determine the extent of God's blessings on us. True _____ False _____

6. The church glorifies God when it (select the proper response):

    _____ (1) Engages in worship

    _____ (2) Builds new buildings

    _____ (3) Stays busy

    _____ (4) Shows its character as God's redeemed people

7. According to the text, praise to God comes primarily from _____ and _____. (Supply the two sources.)

Answers:
1. (3); 2. (3); 3. False; 4. (1); 5. False; 6. (4); 7. Christ, the church.

Church of St. John at Ephesus. The church was built over the traditional site of the apostle's tomb.

7

Life in the
Body of Christ

Ephesians 4:1-24

With 4:1, the second part of Ephesians begins. In the first part, Paul praised God for the greatness of God's redemption—a redemption conceived in eternity, executed in Jesus Christ, and resulting in the creation of the community of believers. The community is the new humanity, God's new people, that transcends the divisive structures of an evil world and is made one in Christ. In the second part of Ephesians, chapters 4—6, Paul exhorted his readers to live according to what God had done and was doing in their midst.

The Unity of the Body (4:1-6)

For Paul, Christian ethics arose out of theology and was related closely to it. He insisted on a unity of belief and behavior. "Therefore" in 4:1 calls attention to the material in the first three chapters and emphasizes the essential unity between belief and behavior.

The believers' lives are to be shaped by God's own purpose, not by anything else. Culture, practical considerations, personal ambitions and prejudices are not to be allowed to thwart this purpose. Only one thing matters supremely, and that is what God is doing in his church.

The man who was about to address his exhortations to the church gave a revealing autobiographical note. He was "a prisoner for the Lord' ' (v. 1). The Greek preposition *en* can be translated as in, making the phrase read: a prisoner in the Lord. Paul was indeed a prisoner. His imprisonment, however, was not a reason for shame. He was in jail because of his service for his Lord. As a prisoner, he was in the Lord; his imprisonment occurred because of his relationship to Jesus Christ.

The man who had paid the price for his commitment had a right to ask others to join him in commitment to Christ. No leader has a right to ask others to do what he is not willing to do or to make sacrifices that he is not willing to make. One reason why our appeals often fall on deaf ears is because people perceive the appeals' hollowness and hypocrisy. Sometimes, we want people to do what we are not willing to do and to make sacrifices that we are not willing to make. Not so with Paul. He had put everything on the line in order to be a channel of God's redemptive purpose. That purpose was, and is, to create a new people united in one body by his love.

Based on his exposition of what God had done, Paul exhorted his readers to "lead a life worthy of the calling" to which they had been called (v. 1). Primarily, as can be seen from the following passage, Paul had in mind the life of the believer in relationship to fellow Christians. Christians live in a community created by God. Relationship to the community determines the believer's way of life.

The "calling" or vocation to which the believers had been called essentially was to be the body of Christ. By God's call—his initiative of grace and his saving work—the readers had been integrated into the body of Christ. Their thoughts and actions were to measure up to this high vocation.

The Qualities That Maintain Unity

What are those qualities that will enable believers to live together as God desires and to give testimony to his mighty work? Paul enumerated four. They are lowliness, meekness, patience, and forebearance (v. 2), which express God's love that believers have received.

These words all are given their meaning in the Christian community by our Lord's life. "Lowliness"—or, perhaps humility—is not an expression of weakness but of strength. This quality is exemplified best by Jesus who voluntarily surrendered his status as sovereign Lord to become one with us, walk with us, identify with us, and suffer for us.

People who are secure in their own persons and in their relationship with God do not lord it over their brothers and sisters. Persons secure in this way identify with others and share their weaknesses and their needs. People marked by lowliness or humility do not think about personal glory but about the welfare of those whom Christ loves.

Baptismal pool in the Double Church of Mary in Ephesus

"Meekness" also can be translated gentleness. Meekness is the opposite of roughness and bad temper.

"Patience" describes the person who does not give up on another when he or she is weak and erring. The impatient person cannot tolerate the faults and failures of others. When another person does not measure up, the impatient individual severs relationships with that person and becomes harsh and judgmental.

Believers are to forebear "one another in love" (v. 2). This injunction means that love is to be the governing force in all their relationships with one another. Love keeps forebearance from being solely negative. We are not just to put up with one another when relationships are difficult. We are to reach out actively to others in love when they are difficult to live with. Some church members feel that they are acting nobly when they assume a neutral attitude in the midst of conflict. Jesus did not say, "Blessed are the neutral." He said, "Blessed are the peacemakers" (Matt. 5:9). Believers are to be engaged actively in maintaining a relationship of love in the body of Christ.

Unity was viewed by Paul as something given. The Spirit's presence is one of the central characteristics of the body of Christ. The Spirit gives unity, but believers have a responsibility; they are to be zealous in maintaining this precious gift of the Spirit.

The Source of Unity
That Paul drew on a confession or a hymn in 4:4-6 is agreed generally. In this passage, Paul enumerated those factors that make for unity in the church.

"There is one body" (v. 4). Christ does not have many bodies. Everyone who believes in him is a member of the one body. The body is led, motivated, and empowered by "one Spirit." A different Spirit does not exist for every denomination or splinter group. Wherever believers in Christ are gathered together, they constitute the body of Christ in that place led by the one Spirit of God. Believers also have "one hope" or destiny. A separate heaven does not exist for each denomination.

Furthermore, only "one Lord" reigns, and this Lord is Jesus Christ (v. 5). All genuine believers are in service to the same Lord. Only "one faith" is sufficient. Faith does not mean intellectual assent to a body of beliefs. It means personal trust and confidence in Jesus as Lord. All who are members of the body have the same kind of trust in Jesus. And all believers share "one baptism." Paul, of course, did not have form in mind. All scholars today generally agree that baptism in the first century was by immersion. What Paul wrote about was baptism as public confession of faith in Jesus Christ. This was one of the main aspects of New Testament baptism.

Moreover, Paul recognized only "one God" who is the Father of all believers (v. 6). He is "above all," supreme ruler of the universe. He acts "through all"; whatever is done is accomplished by him rather than by the people he uses. This means that the church should engage in no cult of the personality, no glorifying of individuals. This is one of the primary causes of divisions in the body. This one God also lives through his Spirit "in all"—in all believers (v. 6).

The Growth of the Body (4:7-16)

In the preceding verses, Paul stressed the members' responsibility for the unity of Christ's body, the church. In verses 7-12, he noted the differences among the members of the body. But he also showed how these differences are to serve God's purpose of unity. The members differ in the roles they are to play as individuals in their service to Christ's body. Each believer has a definite function in God's new people.

The Source and Purpose of the Gifts

"But grace was given to each of us" (v. 7). In this instance, "grace" is not saving grace. Rather, it is the expression of God's love in giving gifts to his children so that they can be useful to his purpose for the church, God's new people.

Several ideas are involved in Paul's statement. Above all, he knew that God is the source of whatever gift each member has. When we recognize that what we have comes from God, we have no room for pride. He does not give us gifts to elevate us above others. The purpose of those gifts is to equip us to serve others.

Another important idea is that all members of the church are recipients of God's grace. Each one has a unique gift; he or she may have many gifts. This implies responsibility. If God has given us gifts, we have the responsibility of recognizing and accepting gratefully those gifts. Furthermore, we have the responsibility of using them according to God's purpose for his church.

Moreover, our gifts are not paltry or limited. They are the kinds of gifts that only the Christ (Messiah) can give. Or, as Paul put it, this special gift or grace from God is to be measured by "Christ's gift" (v. 7).

Then Paul quoted from the Old Testament (Ps. 68:18) to underline the fact that Christ's ability to give is limitless and inexhaustible. Paul understood the psalmist's statement to be messianic.

The statement Paul used emphasizes Christ's transcendent sovereignty, a theme that is present elsewhere in Ephesians. He "ascended on high"; furthermore, he "led a host of captives" (v. 8).

The question is: Who were these captives who were led as prisoners in the triumphant Messiah's train? Taking our cue from other references in Ephesians, we understand that these were the spiritual powers that held people in slavery.

Ascent implies a prior descent. The Messiah's descent mentioned by Paul in verses 9-10 was the incarnation. "The lower parts of the earth" (v. 9) probably should be understood as *The New English Bible* translates: "to the lowest level, down to the very earth."

The emphasis in Paul's discussion, however, was not on descent, but on ascent. The triumphant, reigning Christ gives grace to all members of his body and distributes gifts among them.

The gifts vary, but they come from the same source. They are distributed according to the will and wisdom of the church's Lord. The gifts are given for the same ultimate purpose. They are expressions of the body's unity, therefore, and should not be used to set members of the body against each other.

Verse 11 contains one of the lists of gifts appearing in the Pauline correspondence. Others may be seen in 1 Corinthians 12:28-30 and in Romans 12:6-8. Note that no gift is identical with another. The ministry of the church had not become formal and rigid. The Lord's will for each particular congregation determined that body's ministry. This is in contrast to most contemporary Christian groups where the kinds of ministries are fixed by tradition and have little flexibility. No Pauline list can be taken as normative and exhaustive. Paul's theology would not allow this. Each list is representative.

In the list found in Ephesians, the gifts were limited to those related to the proclamation of the word. Moreover, Paul did not list the gifts in the abstract, but he referred to persons who were bearers of the gifts.

The first group listed in 4:11 is the "apostles." When Paul mentioned apostles in a list, he put them first. Here, the meaning was restricted to those persons who were commissioned directly by the Lord to be witnesses to the resurrection. Paul considered himself to be a member of this group.

By the nature of the case, no more apostles could be selected. For the church in later generations, the function of the apostles has been performed by the New Testament, in which the apostolic witness is preserved.

The second group mentioned in verse 11 is "prophets." The prophet was a person who received a word from the Lord and proclaimed it to the people. Unfortunately, in modern English "prophet" generally means one who predicts the future. This is not the biblical sense. The prophet might deliver a word about the past, present, or future; the only distinguishing characteristic was that the word was from God. Since the church could not live, decide, or act apart from God's word, the prophet was absolutely essential to the life of the church.

"Evangelists" were probably the missionary, itinerant preachers of the gospel. Their main task may have been to call people to a decision for Christ, but their work was not limited necessarily to this. They also could preach to the congregation.

"Pastors and teachers" are linked by the syntax and may refer to the same function. A part of the pastors' shepherding responsibility was to instruct believers. The pastor was the church's primary teacher. He still should be.

The diverse gifts have one unifying purpose. The Lord of the church has given to the church persons graced by these essential gifts in order that his purpose for the body may come to fruition.

The function of the persons given to the church is to prepare the body's members or "to equip the saints" (v. 12). "Saints" has the common Pauline meaning. It is the name given to all believers.

But what are the saints to be prepared for? The saints are to be prepared for "the work of the ministry." Probably, no comma should be placed after "saints." In other words, the church is the minister. The purpose of the various ministries is to prepare the church to be the body through which her Lord performs his ministry in the world.

The church has no role for spectators. Each person has his or her own responsibility to contribute to the wholeness of the ministry of Christ's body. As long as any one member of the body is not functioning properly, the whole is crippled and unable to perform its ministry completely.

Growth Toward Maturity

How long is this period of preparing the saints to continue? Paul gave the answer: Preparation will go on until complete maturity is achieved. What is the standard by which maturity is measured? The answer is: The maturity of the Christ who is the head of the church (v. 13). His purpose is that the body be as mature as the head.

Paul used various words and phrases to describe the maturity he had in mind. One of these was "unity" (v. 13). For Paul, disunity in the church was a characteristic sign of childishness or immaturity. (See 1 Cor. 3:1-4.)

But unity proceeds from a certain source. It has specific characteristics. Unity results from having the "faith and . . . the knowledge of the Son of God" (v. 13). This phrase is ambiguous. Did Paul mean faith in and knowledge of the Son of God possessed by believers? Or, was it Jesus' own faith and knowledge that is the measure of the church's maturity. Most translators have chosen the first option. The second, however, is certainly a real possibility. The church's faith and knowledge are to reach such a level that they are identical to that possessed by Christ.

The church is to attain "to mature manhood" (v. 13). This is "measured by nothing less than the full stature of Christ" (NEB).

Paul stated negatively the purpose of the church's equipping ministries: "so that we may no longer be children" (v. 14). Paul saw the church as moving from immaturity to maturity, from childishness to responsible adulthood.

What is the characteristic of childishness? The one mentioned by Paul is instability (v. 14). From the beginning, Christians had to live out their faith in a world of opposing ideas. These ideas often were attractive and convincing. Paul did not specify the nature of the ideas that opposed faith in Christ. No doubt they were pagan in their origin and nature. One thing we may say for sure. Paul did not have in mind splitting theological hairs in the way that has divided Christians since his time. What he meant were those things which oppose faith in Christ and the union of love in his body.

Like a rudderless ship on a stormy sea, immature believers are the prey to all the doctrines devised by crafty people to turn them from their destiny (v. 14). Paul did not describe the teachings, but he gave a harsh description of the persons teaching false ideas. They were "cunning." Their intent was to trick and deceive.

By contrast, believers are to speak the "truth in love" (v. 15). What is the basic distinction between the true and the false teacher? The difference begins with the attitude toward the other members of Christ's body. The genuine teacher loves people and wants to help them. The false teacher pursues his own ambitions and exploits people for his own ends.

In the context of loving teaching, people can move toward the goal which God has for the church. With the help of shepherding teachers, the body can grow toward a maturity that equals the maturity of the head.

Verse 16 is one of the most difficult verses in the whole New Testament to translate. From most of the translations, the important points emerge. Let us note these points.

First, the body is dependent completely on the head for both its unity and its growth. Second, the body's unity is of paramount importance. As the physical body is united by joints and ligaments, so must the members of Christ's body be united to each other. Third, each individual part has a responsibility for the growth of the whole. Growth takes place as each member of the body "is working properly"—is performing its specific function. One of the main problems with most churches is that too many of their members are maimed, atrophied, or idle.

The goal is the "growth" or building up of the whole body. Here Paul mixed his metaphors, moving from the realm of physiology to the realm of construction. The idea, however, is clear. The growth of the whole is the aim of each part.

Far too many Christians try to function in isolation from their brothers and sisters. Too many splinter groups form, each purer in its own eyes than the other. The believer can be in the purpose of Christ only when that person sees his or her own place in the context of all that Christ is doing in

Remains of the Temple of Artemis in Ephesus. It was one of the seven wonders of the world.

and among his people.

Personal Morality in the Body (4:17-24)

Paul's first concern in Christian ethics arose out of his ecclesiology, his concept of the church. His ethic was primarily a social ethic, related to the way people were to live together in the new community created by God.

But Paul also was aware of the importance personal morality has. To be sure, a close connection exists between personal and social ethics. Paul never lost sight of the fact that each individual is to be understood in the light of that person's incorporation into God's new people.

The Radical Break with the Old Immoral Life

Paul believed that in redemption, God had created a new people who were to have a totally new way of life. The problem was that the Gentiles among this new people had encountered the gospel in a pagan environment. Their background had not prepared them for their new way of life. They still were pulled by their past and pressured by their pagan surroundings. The Gentiles had great difficulty in understanding the demands of their new life and great difficulty in resisting the attractions of their old.

Paul's first concern was to insist that the Gentiles' break from the past must be radical and total. He wrote: "You must no longer live as the Gentiles do" (v. 17). "Gentiles" here is synonymous with pagans. Paul's description of the pagan life in his day was dark and forbidding. Gentiles lived "in the futility of their minds" (v. 17). Other contemporary non-Christian writers might laud Rome's greatness, men of letters' achievements, and life's goodness and richness. But Paul wrote that it was "futile." Pagans were involved in frustrating efforts to pursue meaningless goals.

The cause of all this was clear: the pagans' lack of understanding and their alienation. The two were related closely. Nonbelievers did not know how to plan, choose, or act because they were ignorant (v. 18). People who are ignorant are in darkness. People in darkness cannot see where they are going; they stumble and turn without any sense of direction.

Pagans were cut off from "the life of God" (v. 18). This explained their darkness, because God is the only source of light by which people can live meaningful lives. Paul already had described this situation in those poignant words, "having no hope and without God in the world" (2:12).

Paul clearly placed the responsibility for their sad and tragic state of affairs on the nonbelievers themselves. He believed in malignant and evil spiritual powers, which he generally referred to as flesh, sin, authorities.

But his theology did not relieve people's personal responsibility for evil. A phrase popularized by a comedian went: "The devil made me do it." Paul would have rejected strongly this cover-up for human moral irresponsibility.

The darkness and alienation characteristic of the pagan life was due to the Gentiles' "ignorance" (v. 18). However, the Gentiles were responsible for their ignorance. God had not hidden from them; they had refused the knowledge of God. (See Rom. 1:19-21.) They had chosen to reject the light that had come to them. Paul emphasized the Gentiles' personal responsibility for their darkened condition by adding the phrase "due to their hardness of heart" (v. 18). The light of the knowledge of God had come to them, but it had not been able to penetrate the defenses they had thrown up against it.

Thus, the Gentiles had become "callous" or insensitive, and they had "given themselves up to licentiousness" (v. 19). The question, therefore, was not the same as that of a person who was morally sensitive, who desired to do right, but who occasionally stumbled and fell. The answer to that kind of problem was—and is—the grace of a forgiving God. The Gentiles' problem was much more fundamental. It was complete moral insensitivity that made possible unbridled abandonment to all kinds of immorality.

The lack of restraint so characteristic of pagan society was highlighted by the phrase translated "greedy to practice every kind of uncleanness" (v. 19). The pagans had an insatiable lust for immorality that could not be satisfied. One immoral excess simply led to others.

The Old Nature and the New

Morally, Christ stands at the other pole from the lust and license that ruled unregenerated humanity. In his life and in his teachings, Christ represented the highest and best in morality. Paul did not know personally and specifically about his Christian readers' training. He assumed, however, that they had received some moral and ethical instruction and that this instruction had been harmonious with the truth of Jesus (v. 21).

One of Paul's major emphases was that the moment of decision for Christ was a moment in which a new creation took place. The break with the past was to be total and radical. Life was to go in a totally different direction.

Paul believed that redemption was the result of God's sovereign activity. But this did not in any way lessen the believers' responsibility for the direction of their own lives. This is one of the thorniest problems of Christian (and Pauline) theology. What is the relationship between God's sovereignty and human freedom? The Christian community has been split many times over arguments about this issue.

Paul seemed to hold the two in tension. His answers depended on the question. Sometimes the question revolved around the possibility of people saving themselves by their works. Paul's consistent answer to this was that persons are saved solely by grace. Sometimes the question was the opposite. Have the people whom God has saved no responsibility for the moral direction of their lives? Paul's consistent answer was that God's people are responsible for their moral decisions and actions.

In 4:22-23, Paul seemed to place the responsibility squarely on believers for their actions. This passage contains three verbs. Two of these are found in the aorist tense. They are "put off" (v. 22) and "put on" (v. 24). The aorist tense emphasizes the decisive and inclusive nature of the posture which Paul urged on his readers. They were to put off the old nature and to put on the new nature once and for all.

The old nature belonged to the believers' old life before God had encountered them in Christ. The old life had been corrupt and decaying, the victim of "deceitful lusts" (v. 22). "Deceitful lusts" are evil desires that promise, but they do not fulfill. They promise happiness and satisfaction; they promise life and fulfillment. But they lead to frustration, misery, and death.

The new nature is totally different. It has been "created after the likeness of God" (v. 24). This phrase is reminiscent of the Old Testament story of creation. Humanity had been created in the image, or after the likeness, of God. But as a result of sin, human nature has become evil and corrupted. In redemption, God creates the new person after his likeness.

We could go far afield in discussing the meaning of the phrase, "created after the likeness of God" (v. 24). Here, however, Paul's concern was moral. Anything created after God's likeness participates in his character, and his character is marked by "true righteousness and holiness" (v. 24).

The image in the verbs we have been discussing comes from the removal of old, dirty clothes and the donning of the new, clean ones. Some people believe that such a metaphor was suggested by early baptismal practices. Even at this time, the newly baptized converts may have been clothed in white robes after they came out of the water as one expression of their new life.

When Paul wrote, "Be renewed in the spirit of your minds" (v. 23), he used the present tense, a distinction that is not clear in the Revised Standard Version's translation. While the other two actions are done once for all time, being renewed is something that takes place constantly in the believer's life. Renewal is ongoing.

This repeated renewal often has been misunderstood by Christians who believe they can be sanctified in one fell swoop. They go to the altar to dedicate themselves completely to God, believing that they will solve their spiritual problems and will resolve their spiritual struggles forever. But such a decision suffices only for the moment. At each step along life's journey, the Christian must be renewed. Renewal, ideally, takes place at every instance of the Christian's existence.

Paul emphasized the inwardness of the believer's renewal with the phrase "in the spirit of your minds" (v. 23). This is probably his way of describing the innermost core of a person's existence. Renewal is from the inside out, not the reverse.

So, Paul was concerned about outward actions. He enjoined believers to put off the old way of life and to put on the new person. But he also was concerned about the inward springs of behavior. In this he was in harmony with his Lord who emphasized that genuine morality begins with a pure heart.

Responsible Living in the Body of Christ

When we call people church members, we generally mean something different from anything found in the New Testament. We usually mean that their names are on the roll of the church. This may be the only thing that distinguishes them as members. Many of them never assemble to worship with their fellow Christians. Many of them do not share with their brothers and sisters the responsibility of supporting the church's ministry. But if you ask them about their church relationship, they will affirm that they are church members.

In Paul's writings, however, a church member was a functioning part of the body. That is what made a person a member. The Christian was a part of God's new people in the same way that an arm or a leg is united to the human body to help it to function.

Paul did not conceive, nor could he conceive, of an individual Christian apart from relationship in the church. His words of admonition always were addressed to believers in the context of their relationship to the body of Christ. Each member had responsibility. All believers were responsible for one another. They all were responsible to contribute to the function of the whole body by doing what they were supposed to do as members.

In our day, our concept of gifts and responsibility has been conditioned by our rigid ecclesiastical forms. To a great extent, we assume that the official ministers of the church have gifts and are responsible for using them. Many members, however, seem to feel that they do not have to take seriously the question of their own gifts.

According to Paul's theology, each one has been given a gift to be used to complete the body's function. If this is true, then every member must ask seriously: "What is my gift?" And, having discovered the gift, the Christian is to exercise it in a community of love for the welfare of the whole body.

Personal Learning Activities

1. Paul saw little relationship between belief and behavior.
   True _____ False _____
2. According to Dr. Tolbert, only one thing matters supremely in our world. From the following list, choose the correct answer.
   _____ (1) What I want personally
   _____ (2) What God is doing in his church
   _____ (3) How strong the nation is
   _____ (4) When Christ will come again
3. Match the two lists, linking term with definition:
   _____ (1) Calling   (a) Humility
   _____ (2) Lowliness   (b) Refusal to give up
   _____ (3) Meekness   (c) Actively reaching out in love
   _____ (4) Patience   (d) Vocation as the people of God
   _____ (5) Forebearance   (e) Gentleness
4. Paul enumerated seven factors that make for unity in the church. Choose the proper responses from the list.
   _____ (1) One body   _____ (6) One Lord
   _____ (2) One denomination _____ (7) One faith
   _____ (3) One Spirit   _____ (8) One baptism
   _____ (4) One Hope   _____ (9) One God
   _____ (5) One Bible   _____ (10) One confession of faith
5. According to Paul, God's purpose in giving persons to his church was for those persons to (select the correct response):
   _____(1) Do most of the work
   _____(2) Equip the saints for ministry
   _____(3) Give directions
   _____(4) Serve the saints
6. Paul compared the church to a _____ . (Choose the proper answer.)
   (1) Business
   (2) Team
   (3) Military unit
   (4) Body
7. Paul placed great stress on personal morality.
   True _____ False _____

Answers:
1. *False*; 2. (2); 3. (1)d, (2)a, (3)e, (4)b, (5)c; 4. (1), (3), (4), (6), (7), (8), (9); 5. (2); 6. (4); 7. *True.*

The great theater at Ephesus where the angry mob took Paul's two friends (Acts 19:29)

8

Christian Morality in Action

Ephesians 4:25 to 5:20

In previous passages, Paul wrote about morality in general, in terms of principles and attitudes characteristic of God's new people. In this section, Paul made some practical and concrete applications of those principles.

Actions that Affect Others (4:25-32)

What does it mean to strip off the old nature? To do so means that one has finished with double-dealing, with deception, and with dishonesty. The lie is no longer an accepted tool to be used in relationship with others.

Paul did not believe that "falsehood" (v. 25) had any place in the believer's life. Rather, he admonished everyone to "speak the truth with his neighbor," using a quotation from Zechariah 8:16. The truth for Paul transcended the realm of the factual, although this would be included. The truth was above all the reality that had been discovered in Christ. The believer had emerged from the realm of illusion and deceit into a life of

103

reality and truth.

The reason Paul gave for speaking the truth is the relationship which believers have with one another as members of Christ's body. That body's health depends on openness and trust. The body is injured by dishonesty which breeds suspicion and hostility.

In the second injunction, Paul warned against allowing anger to lead one into sin (v. 26). Anger is one of the most destructive forces in human society. It has been extremely harmful to the life of the church.

We should recognize, first of all, that Paul did not command people to be angry. But he did recognize that anger would arise when people were related closely to one another. Various versions interpret the meaning of the statement correctly when they translate: if you do get (become, are) angry.

Paul recognized that anger can become obsessive and dominate a person's life. Therefore, he gave practical advice: "Do not let the sun go down on your anger" (v. 26). The believer is not to nurture and feed his anger. To nurture anger causes it to become corrosive and destructive. From Paul's point of view, we are to take steps to deal with our anger immediately. We are not to allow the day of anger to pass before anger is resolved so that we do not sin by holding a grudge.

Paul added: "And give no opportunity to the devil" (v. 27). Basically, the term "devil" means slanderer, and so it is appropriate. Anger is dangerous because it gives the devil an opportunity to do his work. More often than not, anger leads to slander, which is the devil's work.

Dishonesty in social intercourse is not a part of the believer's new life. Neither is dishonesty in gaining a livelihood (v. 28). Stealing belonged to that old way of life that had been put off. Honest labor was characteristic of the new nature that had been put on. All honest work is commendable and can be an expression of a Christian's attitude. Paul raised manual labor to the highest possible level. In our so-called Christian culture, people who labor with their hands often are looked down on and relegated to the inferior classes; this is a regrettable and an erroneous judgment.

The major reason Paul gave for Christians' engaging in honest work to earn money is interesting. We should work to support our families. We should work to avoid being a burden on others. These are good Christian reasons for earning an honest living. But Paul gave the highest Christian motive of all. Believers should earn an honest income in order to be able to "give to those in need" (v. 28).

Next, Paul set forth the general principle that is to govern the believer's conversation. The Christian is to refrain from "evil talk" (v. 29). As the context shows, this means more than filthy or foul language, although such language would be included. Evil talk is destructive and harmful to others; this primarily seems to be the view here.

Christian conversation is characterized by its positive effect. Its purpose is to *edify,* to build up, and to help other people (v. 29). It "fits the occasion" because it is designed to meet the needs of others, whatever those needs may be. Christian conversation encourages the despairing; it is the word of love to the lonely, the word of grace to the guilty.

The purpose of Christian talk is seen in the phrase, "that it may impart grace to those who hear" (v. 29). The word "grace" can describe what is charming or attractive. But we probably should think of it here in terms of God's grace. The believer's talk can be an instrument of God's power, help, and forgiveness.

Not only does evil talk harm people. *It also grieves the Spirit of God* who is present in God's children (v. 30). The Holy Spirit is described as the seal by which God authenticates his people until the day of their complete redemption.

Many people watch their language in the church building because they think of it as God's house, the place where God is. This was not Paul's thinking. For Paul, each believer is a temple of God's Spirit. Wherever the Christian is, the Spirit is there. The believer always should be aware, therefore, that his or her whole life is lived in the Spirit's presence. What the believer says on the golf course or in the barber shop or in the grocery store should be just as responsible as what that person says in the church building—perhaps even more so.

Paul's teaching about the misuse of the tongue reached a climax in verse 31. Notice the movement in the catalogue of vices. The list begins with those inward attitudes that are evil and destructive and moves to their outward expression. "Bitterness and wrath and anger" (v. 31) describe the inward poisons that erupt in "clamor and slander." When bad feelings toward others are harbored and allowed to fester, they result in clamor— loud and abusive attacks.

"Slander" translates a word that in other contexts may be rendered blasphemy. Speech is blasphemy if directed against God. Words constitute slander if directed against another human being. Paul had in mind the common practice of reviling other people who are the objects of our bitterness and anger.

"Malice" is a summary word which includes all the words in the preceding list in verse 31. It describes a person's hostile attitude toward another human being. Malice is that attitude that makes us desire and work for another's downfall and hurt.

The quality of the believer's life is new and different. It is expressed in kindness, compassion, and forgiveness (v. 32). These stand in direct contrast to the hostile, hateful, and spiteful attitudes Paul had mentioned.

The new attitude toward others arises out of one source—God's incredible expression of love toward us. We are not to forgive our brother because he deserves it. We are to forgive him "as God in Christ forgave" us (v. 32), and we were not deserving of that forgiveness.

The Life That Is Shaped by Love (5:1-7)

Paul stated the moral demand on believers in the strongest possible terms: "Be imitators of God" (5:1). The statement is no stronger, however, than the demand uttered by Jesus in the Sermon on the Mount: "You, therefore, must be perfect, as your heavenly Father is perfect" (Matt. 5:48). The imperative under which God's people live is not less than that embodied in God's own character.

The goal of our striving, the standard by which we are judged, is not some other poor, weak person. Our standard is nothing less than God's own character, which is holy love.

Obviously, in some areas we cannot imitate God. So we well might ask the question: How are we to understand Paul's injunction? Paul went on to broaden the scope of the demand. Believers are to "walk in love" (v. 2). "Walk" here stands for conduct. The term embraces attitudes, acts, and relationships. The specific idea is related to the believer's life in the body of Christ. The Christian's total life is to be determined by love for brothers and sisters in Christ.

Again we well might ask the question: What is love? This is an elusive word used in so many contexts. It has a thousand meanings in the human vocabulary, but it has a central meaning in biblical texts. Love is not left undefined; it is given content by a specific person and a specific act.

Love Exemplified by Christ

When the New Testament deals with the subject of love (*agape*), it refers to the love that God expressed through Christ. Paul's concept of love was consistent with this New Testament understanding. What does it mean to walk in love? Our understanding of that way of living arises out of our experience of Christ's own love. His life was determined totally by his love for us.

We should notice that Paul did not think of Christ as a pawn in some game that God played. The events and actions of the incarnation were not determined by some kind of divine mechanical force. What Christ did had only one reason. He loved us.

Self-giving love explains God's eternal plan of redemption mentioned in Ephesians 1:5. The coherence between the Father and Son was produced by love. That same love gave birth to God's redemptive purpose and is the force that lies behind its execution. In this connection, note the flaw in all positions based on determinism, such as extreme Calvinism. What God does is not explained basically by sovereign election. Election must be understood in terms of love, or it becomes lifeless, cold, mechanical, and—in some instances—monstrous.

One event in the life of Christ defined this love supremely. This event was the cross—Christ "gave himself up for us" (5:2). Once again, note that the initiative lay with God. Jesus' death was not something God forced on or did to Christ for us. Christ's self-giving was something that God did in Christ for us. The purpose of Christ's self-giving is not to be found in a force that pushed Christ from behind. The purpose is to be found in a force that pulled him from the future. He died in order to redeem us.

We must understand that Christian love is not a sentiment or a feeling. Love in biblical terms primarily is doing. This is not to say, to be sure, that the person who acts in love is devoid of feeling. But we must rescue our concept of Christian love from the realm of sentiment. Love is something we do.

Paul completed his statement with a phrase that described God's response to Christ's self-giving love. This response emphasized the unity between the two. To describe God's response, Paul made use of ideas and words from the Old Testament that were engrained deeply in him. The terminology is found in such passages as Genesis 8:21 and Leviticus 1:9.

In the Old Testament, a sacrifice that was acceptable to God was said to be like a sweet perfume ascending to his nostrils. This anthropomorphism was typical of the Old Testament. It was an attempt to describe God in human terms. It meant that the sacrifice was pleasing to God.

While the phrase is rooted in the Old Testament, a distinctly New Testament idea emerges in the context. What God expects of his new people is not grain and animal offerings. He desires acts of self-giving love—lives offered up for others consistent with Christ's own act of love.

Immorality to Be Shunned

The ethical demand of the Christian life has been stated in positive terms. Paul also found it necessary to state it in negative terms. Theoretically, this should not be necessary. The demand of love is all-inclusive. As is stated elsewhere in the Bible, on it "depend all the law and the prophets" (Matt. 22:40).

But love or grace can be misunderstood so easily. Paul had to fight against an interpretation of grace that failed to take Christian morality seriously. Therefore, Paul felt compelled to mention the kinds of things not appropriate to a life of love. The first is "fornication" (v. 3), a term that refers to sexual immorality in general. Next is a prohibition against "all impurity"; or, perhaps for greater emphasis we should translate, impurity of every kind.

The third evil mentioned, "covetousness" (v. 3), moves from the overt expression of evil to the inner springs out of which immoral actions arise. The word may refer to unlicensed sexual desire. More often, however, it refers to the inordinate or idolatrous drive to gain material possessions.

No doubt the common table talk in pagan society involved a great deal of lewd discussion about sex and general immoral practices which were the order of the day. The same is true of our society today where much boasting takes place about adulterous and other illicit sexual relations. Paul instructed Christians not to follow these practices. They were not to commit immoral acts. They should not even discuss them as possibilities (v. 3).

Clearly, Paul did not mean that the Christian community is not to discuss sex and sexual morality. That is exactly what he did here. He also discussed sexual morality in many other places, especially in Corinthians. But our concerns are to be Christian concerns. Believers need to help each other gain a Christian moral perspective.

Believers are to be moral both in actions and in speech. Their conversation is to be Christian. Paul, therefore, warned his readers against conversation that is filthy, silly, and ribald (v. 4). The word translated "levity" in the Revised Standard Version means, in a good sense, humor; in a bad sense, the term means ribaldry, low jesting.

Paul did not forbid a healthy sense of humor. Indeed, he wrote in Colossians 4:6: "Let your speech always be gracious, seasoned with salt." Most interpreters take this statement to mean that the believer's speech is not to be dull and drab. Humor, however, can take the low road or the high one. The Christian's choice is to walk the high road, always following the path of love in his or her conversation. Gaiety and humor are part of the Christian life. But filthy talk is not, and that is what Paul emphasized.

The Christian's tongue is to be used for "thanksgiving" to God rather than filthy talk (v. 4). Thanksgiving is one of the dominant themes in Paul's letters. He believed that gratitude should be one of the basic responses to God's redemptive actions on behalf of his people.

The highest use of our God-given vocal capacity is to praise God. For Christians to use their tongues, which can be employed in thanking God, to engage in filthy, immoral talk is to debase their gift. They also miss an opportunity to give a witness to their new existence in Christ. The person who is thanking God with his tongue is not using it in negative, complaining, harsh, judgmental, and destructive ways.

God's Judgment on Immorality

A hard saying appears in 5:5. Immorality is raised to the most serious level possible: *It keeps a person from inheriting the kingdom of God.* Immoral practices are the sign of the unregenerate person.

Apparently, Paul was concerned about the activity in the Christian community of teachers who perverted the gospel. They taught that immorality was not an issue to people under grace. Paul made a sharp reference to these evil teachers: "Let no one deceive you with empty words" (v. 6). The person who taught that a believer was free to sin had no foundation for his doctrine. This kind of teaching was dangerous and misleading; it was at the opposite pole from the truth in Christ.

Paul went on to admonish his readers: "Do not associate with them" (v. 7). That is, he warned believers not to include the evil and perverse teachers in the Christian fellowship.

The Contrast Between the Old and the New (5:8-20)

Paul's basic concern in the entire section of Ephesians 5:8-20 was to contrast the old pagan way of life with the new life of the Christian converts to whom he was writing. In the pursuit of his purpose, Paul employed the metaphors of darkness and light. These metaphors had been used widely in the realms of philosophy and religion. The Qumran community, for example, had made the metaphors key concepts in its theology. This group of Essenes called themselves children of light in contrast to others, especially other Jews who were thought to be evil and heretical. Paul may have been influenced by this or other contemporary uses of the metaphors. What emerges, however, is the distinctive way he employed them in keeping with his purpose.

Walking in the Light
Paul drew a contrast between "once" and "now" (5:8). He made a sharp distinction between the past and the present. At the time of the readers' conversion, a radical change had taken place in their lives. Not only were the believers new and different, but that difference stood at the opposite extreme from the character of their former lives.

In the past, Paul's readers had been in "darkness." They not only had lived in the sphere of darkness; they had been actual participants in it. They had been part of the darkness itself. Darkness describes their existence that had been in rebellion against God.

But God had changed Paul's readers from darkness to light. He had taken the believers "from the dominion of darkness and transferred [them] to the kingdom of his beloved Son" (Col. 1:13). Therefore, when Paul wrote about the drastic change in the existence of believers he had in mind, first and foremost, God's saving act. Christians had not moved from darkness to light through their own efforts; this change had been brought about by God and God alone.

But, as is so often the case in Paul's writings, the indicative is followed closely by the imperative. Indeed, the indicative makes the imperative possible. God's saving grace places a moral responsibility on believers. So Paul admonished his readers: "Walk as children of light" (v. 8). They were made children of light through God's regenerative power. This placed on them the responsibility—yes, gave them the freedom—to live in harmony with their new existence.

Paul immediately brought the language out of the realm of the abstract. Here we see how Paul's purpose shaped his use of the metaphors. Morality was uppermost in his mind. Walking in the light meant doing what was "good and right and true" (v. 9).

"Good and right and true" must be understood in the context of Ephesians. These words refer to loving one another, forgiving one another, telling the truth, earning an honest living, and refraining from sexual immorality.

Above all, the purpose of the believer's life is to do "what is pleasing to the Lord" (v. 10). We have a responsibility, therefore, to discover what God wants us to do and how he wants us to act. Our text admonishes: "Try to learn what is pleasing to the Lord." "Try to learn" is one way of translating a Greek verb which Paul used in several of his writings. The basic idea here seems to be to learn through testing.

One idea is clear: The will of God is not discerned in the abstract or in a vacuum; it is discerned by people who, first of all, want to please God. Furthermore, God's will is discerned by people who are engaged actively in life, facing its difficult decisions, involved in its demands. As they make decisions, as they engage in actions, as they face problems, they are submitting everything to the test: Will this please God? Paul was confident that people who were involved actively in life and with this kind of purpose would find what God wanted them to do.

Believers are not to participate in the "works of darkness" (v. 11). These are characterized as fruitless. For Paul, life in the Spirit is the only one that bears fruit. The works of darkness lead to decay and death, the opposite of fruitfulness.

The children of light are to "expose" the works of darkness so that they may be seen in their true character and consequences (v. 11). As *The New English Bible* translates, believers are to "show them up for what they are."

But the question arises: How are believers to show up the works of darkness for what they are? One of our tendencies in dealing with immorality is to condemn, criticize, and castigate persons whom we consider to be immoral. But that does not seem to be what Paul had in mind. In fact he wrote: "It is a shame even to speak of the things that they do in secret" (v. 12).

We do not expose evil by our vehement denunciation of evildoers. Rather, we expose evil by our own personal commitment to and our living for the right. By expressing their character as people who have been changed by a holy God, believers shine in the darkness and make visible that which is hidden in it.

The last part of verse 13 is enigmatic and has been subject to many and

The sun shedding its light over the Lower Agora in Ephesus. Paul wrote that Christians act as light to dispel darkness.

varied interpretations. What did Paul mean by the statement, "Anything that becomes visible is light"? Perhaps we should understand the idea to be that light has transforming power. Paul had written that his readers had been darkness, but they had become light. How had they become light? Clearly, this transformation from darkness to light had taken place as the light of God's goodness and grace had shone on them. This interpretation helps us to see the point of the quotation found in verse 14. That Paul introduced this hymnic material in the same way he would introduce a quotation from the Old Testament is interesting. (See Eph. 4:8.)

While interpreters generally agree that the statement in verse 14 is hymnic in form, widespread disagreement exists about the possible source from which it came. Some people think the statement was a Christian hymn used in connection with baptism. This is as good a guess as any.

Paul used the quotation because it contains an affirmation that supports the point he had made. The quotation emphasizes the transforming power of the light that is given to the individual by Christ. When Christ illuminates us, we emerge from the dream world of sleep into the reality of God's life. We are called from the realm of the dead to the transcendent regions of life.

Filled by the Spirit
In his effort to set forth the contrast between the old life and the new, Paul left the metaphors of darkness and light. In verse 15, he moved to the antithesis between wisdom and foolishness.

"Unwise men" are people who live without God and who follow the world's wisdom. No matter how intelligent or competent a person may be judged by the world to be, he or she is a fool if that individual structures life without reference to God.

On the other hand, the wise person determines his or her conduct by the character and purpose of a holy God. That person's life is dependent on God, conforms to his will, and serves him. The contrast between wisdom and foolishness in the biblical sense is contained in verse 17. The wise person understands "what the will of the Lord is" and acts according to this understanding.

Verse 16 states that the wise person makes "the most of the time, because the days are evil." The Greek words in this text are interesting. "Time" translates a word which basically means the opportune moment. "Making the most of" is the Revised Standard Version's translation of a participle that literally means buying up.

The idea in verse 16 seems clear. Believers lived in a world dominated by the forces of corruption. This added urgency to their need to live and act as wise people—people who were under the lordship of God in Christ. Although the days were evil, opportunities presented themselves for

Christian action. When these opportune moments appeared, believers were to seize them, use them, make the most of them. The participle has an intensive prepositional prefix, and so I translated it as buying up. The idea is that God's people are to make intensive and exhaustive efforts to use their opportunities for good.

One expression of foolishness in the first-century world was drunkenness. In ancient society, people did not understand the physiological effects of alcohol. Many of them believed that wine was the drink of the gods. They attributed the effects of alcohol on them to the power of the gods' spirits. Wine often was used in pagan worship. Paul's idea probably is to be understood against this background. He dismissed the pagan ideas and classified drunkenness as "debauchery" (v. 18).

The believer was not to get his inspiration and joy from wine. Rather, what the pagans sought in wine was received by God's people from the Spirit. Therefore, Paul admonished his readers to be "filled with the Spirit" (v. 18). This translation of his admonition can be misleading. Literally, the statement is: Be filled in spirit, or, Be filled by (the) Spirit. If "spirit" here is a reference to the Holy Spirit, as is likely, then the Spirit is not a substance with which we are filled; rather, the emphasis is on God who does the filling. The joy, the consciousness of God, and the peace of the Christian life are imparted *by* the Spirit. The Greek preposition *en* (in) often is used in this instrumental sense.

The other possibility is that the phrase "in spirit" refers to the believer's spirit. Paul's statement then would contrast the fleshly filling with wine and the spiritual filling which should be the desire of believers.

Another point needs to be made: The imperative is in the present tense, which denotes continuous action. Paul was not referring to a one-time experience of being filled by the Spirit. He meant the continuous life of the Spirit from whom the Christian receives his joy and power. We might translate it as: Keep on being filled by the Spirit.

Paul's teaching certainly has a special relevance for American Christians today. We live in an alcohol-oriented society. Far too many people foolishly turn to the bottle to escape from anxiety and to find joy. This is the way of darkness. Many believers find it difficult to move against the powerful tide of social pressure. Not the spirits in a bottle, but the Spirit of the living God brings true joy and meaning to life. We have resources from God that help us face the demands and frustrations of life. We do not need the alcohol crutch.

The joy of the life in the Spirit was expressed appropriately in the music that from the beginning evidently was such a vital part of the Christian assembly. Today, the function of worship is to praise the Lord. A fitting vehicle of corporate worship is singing.

Music in the church is lifted to its proper level in our text. Properly speaking, music is not designed as a showcase for individual talent. Its purpose is to praise the Lord, not to magnify the musician. Paul stressed that in the church's singing, the people are to praise the Lord with all their hearts.

Paul emphasized that music is not solely sentimental and emotional. Much modern religious music has degenerated to this; its sole purpose is to produce a religious feeling. In biblical language, however, the heart is the center of the will and intellect. The great hymns of the church are concerned with the praise of God rather than praise of the worshiper. They make sense—in sharp contrast to the maudlin gibberish sometimes placed in the category of religious music.

Gratitude is related closely to the praise of God (v. 20). Fundamentally, praise is the expression of a grateful heart. Over and over again, Paul emphasized the central place of gratitude in the Christian life. The believer is not to be complaining and negative, but grateful. This is the keynote of the Christian's life. Gratitude is sweeping and all inclusive: Believers are to give thanks "for everything" because their total existence and all their hope for the future are the result of God's saving act, his comforting and helping presence, and his bright promises.

We are to express our gratitude to God "in the name of our Lord Jesus Christ" (v. 20). This means far more than just the ritualistic repetition of a phrase. "Name" stands for the person. We can approach God only because of Jesus Christ's saving deed. Moreover, the reason for our gratitude is what God has done for us through Jesus Christ.

The Tension in Christian Morality

The ethical life of the believer unfolds in relationship to the two polarities of grace and demand. In our passage, Paul emphasized demand. However, we always must keep the two together lest we emerge with a distorted approach to Christian ethics.

Demand without grace results in harsh and unforgiving legalism. Grace without demand results in soft and sentimental permissiveness. The gospel, as Paul understood it, walked the razor's edge between these two extremes.

The word of demand proceeds from a holy God; therefore, it is absolute. To say that the immoral person cannot inherit the kingdom of God is the negative way of putting it. God absolutely does not compromise with evil. The word of demand leads to despair if it is the only one we hear. It means that nobody has any hope, for all of us are sinners. Another word is spoken, however. God is holy; also, he is love. God does not compromise with evil. But he loves, forgives, and accepts the sinner. Nevertheless, his grace is not permissive. God's love calls us to a new commitment to holiness. So we are set once again before the demand. The Christian life is lived in this tension between demand and grace. The first word God addresses to us is the word of grace; the second word he directs to us is his word of demand.

The ethical demand of a holy love is the greatest moral force in the world. If someone who hates us makes a demand on us, that person's efforts to control us are met with resistance. If we are accepted totally by a good person, we find that love pulling us ever higher.

If being loved by someone good does not make us better people, no hope can be held out for us. How much more powerful is the love of a good God! That the incredible awareness of God's love manifested in the cross can give a person permission to be bad is inconceivable. Awareness of God's awesome love pulls us to higher levels of living.

Personal Learning Activities

1. For Paul, truth was defined in terms of (select the proper answer from the list):
   _____(1) Honesty
   _____(2) Directness
   _____(3) Reality
2. In Paul's view, to become angry and to nurture the feeling are acceptable. True _____ False _____
3. The highest Christian motive for honest work, according to Paul, is (choose the proper response from the following list):
   _____(1) To make a living for ourselves
   _____(2) To support our families
   _____(3) To prevent our being burdens to others
   _____(4) To be able to share with those in need
4. The supreme event that defines God's love is the _____.
   (Select the correct response.)
   (1) Creation
   (2) Exodus
   (3) Cross
   (4) Conversion of Paul
5. We expose evil most effectively by our vehement denunciation of it. True _____ False _____
6. What does "making the most of the time" (Eph. 5:16) mean?

Answers:
1. (3); 2. *False*; 3. (4); 4. (3); 5. *False*; 6. *Your answer.*

9

The
Christian Household

Ephesians 5:21 to 6:9

Because of the family's importance in the social structure, various Gentile and Jewish moralists laid down specific guidelines or codes to govern the behavior of family members. The instructions given by Paul, therefore, fell within the general category of codes or tables of family duties with which the ancient world was familiar.

Scholars conjecture that such codes formed a part of the catechetical instruction given to new converts in Christian churches. That such teachings were common in the early churches is seen by their prevalence in the New Testament. In addition to the examples in Ephesians 5:21 to 6:9, similar teachings occur in Colossians 3:18 to 4:1; 1 Timothy 3:4-5,12; 5:14; 6:1-2; Titus 2:1-10; and 1 Peter 2:13 to 3:7.

Paul added a newness to the codes in his letters, for he set them in the context of the Christian faith. He believed that the Christians' total lives were under the lordship of Christ and that all their relationships were to be a testimony to that main relationship.

The Christian home was to be different, therefore, not so much in its structure as in the attitudes that characterized the family's different members. Nothing in the way Paul conceived the structure of the family was new. His view in this regard was not different from Jewish forbears and from many Gentile contemporaries.

A great deal was different, however, in Paul's emphasis on the quality of

Excavation of homes of the wealthy in Ephesus

the relationships in the family structure. Those relationships, as Paul saw them, were transformed by Christ who provided the basic motivations in family relationships.

Many scholars suggest that Paul's teachings about the family members' duties arose in the first place to deal with the possibility of family breakdowns in the churches. Under the impetus of a wrong conception of the believer's new freedom under grace, many people may have tended to throw off their old responsibilities as members of the family. In Corinth, for example, wives denied their husbands the privilege of conjugal relationships or wanted to disavow their marital ties altogether. (See especially 1 Corinthians 7.)

Christian freedom did not produce chaos. An order was maintained in freedom. However, the motivation for that order changed as did the attitudes of the individuals. The motivation was not from without, but from within. Not an external code but the presence of the Spirit within the individual led Christians to orderly and responsible conduct.

Wives and Husbands (5:21-33)

Note that Paul's instruction to wives is a specific example of the general principle he laid down in verse 21. That principle admonishes believers to "be subject to one another." The idea is primarily that of the willingness to defer to others, the readiness to forego one's own ideas or desires out of love for one's brothers and sisters.

In the context of verses 18-21, the primary emphasis is on the conduct of church members in worship. The individual is not to seek to dominate the public expressions of worship. (See 1 Cor. 14:30.) But the principle has a general application to the individual's whole life in the body of Christ. This concept is characteristic of the New Testament as a whole, going back to Jesus' teaching (Mark 10:43). One of the best comments on this attitude was made by Paul in 1 Corinthians: "Love does not insist on its own way" (13:5).

The motivation for such conduct is unusual. The motive is "out of reverence for Christ" (v. 21). The literal translation of the phrase, in the fear of Christ, is probably closer to the thought. This is the only place in the New Testament where this phrase occurs. Usually, Paul wrote about the love of Christ as the motivating force of the Christian life.

But Paul believed that the church lived under the judgment of the Messiah. He also believed that a day of accounting would come. In their relationships to one another, believers eventually would have to answer to their Lord. Therefore, the fear of Christ was appropriate to inculcate a sense of responsibility.

The Husband as the Head

What Paul admonished wives to do in verse 22, therefore, was not something that he expected only of them. He believed that this attitude should characterize the individual in relationship to all others in the church. Wives were not to insist on having their own way as opposed to their husbands.

Wives are to defer to their husbands "as to the Lord" (v. 22). This phrase does not mean that the husband exercises the same authority over the wife as the Lord. The admonition means that the wife's actions are to be determined by her desire to serve her Lord. As we have noted, the believer's whole life is under the lordship of Christ. Everything he or she does is "to the Lord."

Paul believed that God had ordained an order for the family. In this order, the husband is the "head of the wife" (v. 23). Paul simply stated his concept as an assumed fact. He did not seem to feel the need to justify his statement. But he did understand the need to explain his words in Christian terms.

Many people in our contemporary world do not find Paul's concept of God's rule for the home congenial to their thinking. But we need to be fair with him before we argue with him.

Some people have used Paul's ideas in this passage as a springboard to develop positions that are not at all congenial to the original ideas. We cannot emphasize too strongly that the thought of innate male superiority is not here at all.

If we want to see Paul's primary statement on this matter of male and female worth, we have to turn to Galatians 3:28. There, Paul affirmed that in Christ "there is neither male nor female." In the context of that passage, his statement could mean only that old ideas of male worth and female inferiority were uncongenial in the church. In the body of Christ, the old prejudices that made one group feel it was better than the other had been transcended.

Nothing in Ephesians contradicts this concept in Galatians, and much supports it. Paul did not believe that the husband was the head of the wife because he was better or smarter or superior in ability. He simply believed that this design represented God's order for the home.

Furthermore, Paul's concept is clarified by the analogy "as Christ is the head of the church" (v. 23). So the example for the headship of the husband is the headship of Christ. This analogy excludes any notion of swaggering male arrogance; it excludes any idea of insufferable tyranny. The concept of authority, of course, is present. But that concept is a far cry from many of the assumptions that have been based on this text.

We cannot apply anything to the headship of the husband that cannot be deduced from the headship of Christ and, at the same time, be fair to Paul's teaching. So the notion of authority is present, but it is far different in its character from any worldly concept of authority. Paul added another statement about Christ. Christ is also the "Savior" of the body (v. 23). The Greek text contains indications that this statement applies only to Christ and the church, not to the husband and wife.

The Love of the Husband for the Wife

Today, some people may quarrel with Paul's concept of God's order for marriage. To them, his concept may seem to reinforce the woman's subordinate and secondary position in a male-dominated society. In justice, we must recognize that Paul had the family and not society as a whole in mind in this particular context.

Not many will quarrel with Paul's concept of the husband's attitude toward the wife, for the husband is to love his wife.

What Paul meant when he called the husband "the head of the wife" (v. 23) must be interpreted in the light of his view of the husband's role. By calling on husbands to love their wives, Paul asked them to subordinate themselves to their wives in the highest sense. In genuine Christian love, the welfare of the other person always takes precedence over one's own welfare. The needs and desires of that person have a higher priority than one's own needs and desires.

If the husband's function as the head of the wife is expressed in authoritarian or selfish ways, this certainly strays from Paul's interpretation in our text.

In order that no mistake be made about the meaning of love, Paul explicitly stated that husbands are to love their wives "as Christ loved the church" (v. 25). This love was expressed concretely: Christ died for the church. Christ's kind of love will make any sacrifice to secure the welfare of the loved one.

At this point, Paul left the analogy of the husband and wife relationship to describe the ultimate result of Christ's self-giving for the church. He died "that he might sanctify her" (v. 26)—make the church fit to be God's possession. This sanctification has a beginning and an end.

Sanctification's beginning is described by the difficult phrase, "having cleansed her (the church) by the washing of water with the word" (v. 26). Most interpreters feel that this reference is to baptism. Baptism in the New Testament was the moment when the believer made a public confession of faith. Baptism was the means by which the believer's confession was made. Baptism was the moment and the vehicle by which the Christian crossed the line that divided the unbelieving world from the people of God. Not only so, but in texts like this one, baptism could symbolize the cleansing of the individual from his sins. Baptism as a symbol of Christ's activity on behalf of the church would be a natural analogy for Paul to use.

The phrase translated "with the word" has been the subject of much conjecture. To begin with, "word" translates a term that generally means a spoken word. The question is: What spoken word did the writer have in view?

Three major possibilities come to mind. First, "word" may refer to the gospel proclaimed to church members who had responded in faith. Through the word, they had become members of Christ's body. Second, the term may refer to the word spoken at the time of baptism by the administrator. Or, third (and I think most likely), "word" could refer to the public confession made by the believer at the time of baptism.

The third possibility appears to reflect a general practice in the early church. Confessions like the one contained in 1 Corinthians 12:3 generally are believed to have been baptismal confessions. In a text quite reminiscent of the one in Ephesians 5:26, Ananias commanded Paul to "rise and be baptized, and wash away your sins, calling on his name" (Acts 22:16).

The purpose of the Messiah's sanctifying work is "that he might present the church to himself in splendor" (v. 27). "In splendor" translates a word that literally means glorious. This word must be emphasized to bring out the meaning of the text. Christ's purpose is not just to present the church to himself, but his purpose is to present it in its new character that can be described as glorious, splendid, or beautiful.

The glorious character was emphasized further in a negative fashion. When Christ presents the church, it will be without spot or wrinkle, "holy and without blemish" (v. 27). In these words, Paul saw the destiny of the church. As it existed in the world, it was marred by imperfections and faults. But Christ would finish his work. The church would have the character of a perfect offering and, thus, be fit for God's own possession.

The Unity of Husband and Wife

The unity of husband and wife is so complete that they no longer exist as two separate selves. They become one. Husband and wife maintain the uniqueness of their personalities, their individualities. But they become one in love, faithfulness, purpose. That is the point Paul made in verse 28. The husband is to love his wife as he loves his own body. Indeed, in loving his wife, he loves himself, since she is an extension of his own self.

For Paul, this concept had a practical application. An individual shows concern for his or her own body by feeding it and clothing it. As Paul put it, "No man ever hates his own flesh, but nourishes and cherishes it" (v. 29). Obviously, we could point out exceptions to this rule. Some people deliberately abuse, mutilate, or starve their own bodies; but generally, this is not true. In fact, we classify such people as emotionally ill.

No doubt, Christian responsibilities in marriage will be seen differently in different ages and in different cultures. In the first-century world, marriage was seen, at least in part, in basic terms. For most people, life was extremely difficult. Most of their energy was spent in acquiring the absolute necessities to maintain existence.

In ancient society, the situation of unprotected women could be extremely precarious. They depended for life itself on the protection and maintenance provided by the male members of the family. If their men lacked elementary human decency, women could be pushed out of their homes to face the terrifying prospect of starving to death.

The Christian husband was not to act in a harsh, uncaring, inhuman manner toward his wife. He was to nourish and cherish his wife as he did his own body. Concretely, this meant that he was to take the same care to provide her with life's necessities that he showed for himself. Tender, loving support and care were outward expressions of the right relationship to the wife.

For the third time in this passage, Paul invoked the example of Christ to illustrate his meaning. Christ supplies the church's needs (v. 29). All his people, as "members of his body" (v. 30), are objects of his care. None is neglected or omitted from his provision.

The text of Genesis 2:24—"and they become one flesh"—had been in the background of the apostle's thinking all along: "And the two shall become one flesh" (v. 31). This text expresses the vital and indissoluble unity into which husband and wife enter when they marry.

But the text had a double application for Paul, as we see from verse 32. The text referred to marriage. But Paul also understood it to apply to the oneness which existed between Christ and his body, the church.

In this connection Paul wrote, "This mystery is a profound one" (v. 32). "Mystery" here should be understood as a revelation from God, not as something mysterious or unknown. "Great" describes that revelation in terms of its importance or vastness. The *Today's English Version* catches the meaning of the statement with the translation: "There is a deep secret truth revealed in this scripture," a truth which applies "to Christ and the church."

In verse 33, Paul summed up his teachings in the passage. The husband is to love the wife; the wife is to respect the husband. As we have noted, these are nothing more than the proper attitudes of all Christians to one another, applied to the special relationship of marriage.

Children and Parents (6:1-4)

The second important relationship in the home is that between children and parents. Paul believed that this relationship also came under the lordship of Christ. To be a Christian child or a Christian parent was important.

Children were enjoined to "obey your parents" (6:1). That same attitude was to characterize their relationship with both father and mother. Children were to obey parents "in the Lord." This phrase means that their obedience to their parents was only one expression of their commitment to Christ as Lord of their lives.

Note carefully that in Ephesians 6:1-4, Paul was thinking about a Christian home, composed of believing children and parents. He did not deal with the relationship of children to pagan parents.

In Matthew 10:21, Jesus talked about the way the gospel would divide families, setting the father against the believing children and children against believing parents. This situation can arise only because some members of the family decide for God against the will of the others. In this case, naturally, the children have disobeyed their parents.

If a person believes in God, then that individual cannot ascribe complete allegiance to any person, group, or institution. To do so is idolatrous. As we have noted, this problem is not considered in our present text. Paul had in mind the order of the Christian home.

The rightness of obedience is supported by an appeal to the Old Testament Commandment (v. 3). This is unusual in Paul's writings, for he generally made his ethical appeals on some other basis.

The Commandment is described as the first "with a promise" (v. 2). Questions have been raised about the meaning of this assertion. To think of it as the first in point of time would be incorrect. God's command to Abraham in Genesis 12:1, for example, was accompanied by a promise. Perhaps Paul meant that the Commandment under discussion was the first in the Decalogue to involve a promise. We know that exceptions to the promise occur. Good children of believing parents may have short lives. The general principle, however, holds true: Children who heed good parents' instructions will live longer as a group than others. Also, a sound society is based in part on healthy family relationships; in such a society, conditions are created which are conducive to longer life.

Parents also have a special obligation to their children. If children are to obey their parents, parents in turn must be careful about their instructions to their offspring. Instructions must be the kind that will not "provoke [them] to anger" (v. 4). The verb "provoke" evidently refers to creating anger that will result in lasting bitterness and resentment. Some parents are so arbitrary, sporadic, and inconsistent that their authority results in causing brooding resentment and rebellion in their children.

Christian parents are to give their children a Christian rearing. Their "discipline and instruction" must be "of the Lord" (v. 4). This means that both in attitude and content, the discipline of the home should conform to the will of the Lord whose relationship to both parents and children is one of unconditional love.

Slaves and Masters (6:5-9)

In the New Testament world, slaves and servants were considered to be a part of the household. Paul's discussion of slave-master relationships, therefore, is tied to his remarks about other family responsibilities.

Since slavery is so repugnant to most people in our society, we need to evaluate the writer's counsel in the light of the situation faced by believers in the first-century Mediterranean world. First, we need to recognize that Christians constituted a small minority in that world. They were lacking totally in power to change the prevailing political and social situations.

Responsibility for exercising our Christian influence certainly increases as the sphere of opportunity widens. Christians in modern American society have a great responsibility for the evils and injustices of our society. The same kind of responsibility could not have been charged to a Christian in the pagan, tyrannical Roman Empire. Therefore, Paul hardly could have entertained the possibility that Christians should change the structures of an evil society.

Furthermore, the economic system of the free world of Paul's day was totally different from our modern money-based economy. A slave cut off from his master in ancient times did not find a ready market for employment. For many people, the alternative to slavery was starvation.

Paul was not a social reformer in the modern sense. He knew that a pagan society would be corrupt and evil, and he had a negative view of Christian people's possibilities if they lived in a society dominated by sin. Christians had little or no leverage.

But Paul was truly the social reformer in terms of his attitude toward the church. He believed that in the church, the old pagan order had been transcended. God's order of equal worth for all people was the rule for the church. In the church, people were neither "slave nor free" (Gal. 3:28). That this idea would be applied to society as a whole, once the opportunity came, was inevitable.

For Paul, the present order was a passing, doomed one. His advice to Christians was based on this presupposition. They already had been emancipated by the power of God. This gave them the freedom, even in their evil age, to live for their Lord, whatever the circumstances of their lives.

Paul visualized for believers the kind of freedom that is related to Viktor Frankl's documentation in *Man's Search for Meaning*. People like Frankl, enslaved in a Nazi concentration camp, found that a possibility of freedom was left for them. Their lives were controlled completely. But their implacable jailers could not control one area—the area of the prisoners' attitudes. The prisoners were forced to live like slaves, but some of them experienced a freedom that was far greater than any freedom their guards enjoyed.

The Attitude of the Christian Slave

Paul's counsel to Christian slaves was, "Be obedient" (v. 5). This advice certainly contained nothing new or unique. But the new element in the Christian slave's service was his attitude. The slave owner could command physical servitude and could force compliance with his orders, but he could not command the slave's heart.

The limitations, transitory nature, and superficiality of slave ownership were highlighted in the words "earthly masters" (v. 5). This translates a text which literally reads, masters according to the flesh. The masters operated in the realm of the flesh (sarx), a realm that was passing away. They had a certain power in that realm, but that power partook of the nature of the flesh.

The slaves' genuine and eternal allegiance was to Christ (v. 5). They were to use their transient situation of earthly servitude to witness to their eternal relationship with their Lord.

Paul raised the slavery of believers to a higher level. People who were slaves could offer their slavery to their true Lord as a service to him.

Paul used several phrases to describe the Christian slave's free attitude. "With fear and trembling" (v. 5) does not describe their attitude toward their earthly masters. Believers had risen above this. They knew that they did not have to fear people. Their "fear and trembling" expressed their consciousness of their Lord. Their lives were lived before him; ultimately, they answered to him for their actions and attitudes, to no one else.

The superiority of the lordship of Christ is seen in its power to touch the inner core of existence. Christ's lordship affects the will, the heart, the attitude. In this area, slaves could demonstrate where their ultimate allegiance lay.

The Christian slave who used his slavery as a service to Christ is described in both positive and negative ways. Positively, the slave was characterized by "singleness of heart" (v. 5). The Christian slave was to have no mixed motives, no divided allegiance. His service was to be performed "from the heart" (v. 6), or, better, wholeheartedly. The slave's service was not to be grudging, resentful, or dilatory.

Paul also mentioned the negative, unworthy attitudes that the believer should avoid. Christian service was not to be "eye-service" (v. 6). This meant that believers were to be consistent in their work. Since their service was to the Lord, it had the same quality whether they were being watched or not.

Since their concern was to please God, the Christian slaves were not to be motivated by the desire to please people. Persons are motivated by the desire to please people when they expect to get their reward from people.

The slave's ultimate confidence, however, rested in God's justice and not in earthly masters' possible rewards. The Christian slave knew that the only meaningful reward comes from God. The believing slave trusted God to accept his service as an offering and to respond to it in keeping with God's love and power (v. 8).

Paul's counsel has an obvious application to modern society. Whatever we do, we should do it as to the Lord. Our work will be lifted to the highest level if we offer it up as a testimony to our faith in an eternal and loving God.

The Attitude of Christian Masters

The admonitions to Christian slave-owners are much briefer than those to slaves. The reason for this may be simple. The churches included a much larger number of slaves than slave-owners.

Masters were to "do the same" to their slaves (v. 9). They were to relate to their slaves in the spirit and with the attitudes that Paul had described in his counsel to slaves.

"Threatening" had no place in the role of the Christian master (v. 9). "Threatening" was the counterpart of grudging, reluctant service. The believer, whether he was master or slave, must have as his primary concern the welfare of the other. Wholehearted service was to be the slave's Christian response to the master; kindness was to be the master's Christian response to the slave.

The Christian master also was to be aware of the temporary, earthly nature of his relationship to his slave. He was to be concerned primarily about his lasting relationship to his own Lord. Before this Lord, both master and slave stood on the same level ground. They had the same heavenly Lord. The master must respond to the Lord just as the slave must respond to the Lord. The master's earthly superiority did not put him in a favored position with God.

When master and slave appeared before their Lord, Paul affirmed, they would find that he is not prejudiced: "There is no partiality with him" (v. 9). Earthly station and recognition are irrelevant in God's court.

Paul did not visualize a change in the existing social order. His teachings, however, carried the seed that led to the eventual abolition of slavery in lands where Christian principles had enough support to bring changes.

God is not prejudiced. Social distinctions have no place in the church. The division of society into classes determined by sex, race, money, and power is due to society's character as flesh. These divisions mark such a social order as inferior, as rebellious against God, and as doomed. These are teachings that emerge from Ephesians.

That men in later times, like Livingstone and Wilberforce, would understand God's call to them in the light of these principles was inevitable. In their day, God willed the abolition of slavery. This was the word of God to them. We can rejoice that in our time, the Christian principles enunciated by Paul for the church also have had a moderating effect on the evils of society.

The Temporary and the Abiding

We are aware that the forms of social institutions change. A vast difference is evident between the social institutions of the ancient Roman world and those of contemporary American society.

This difference becomes clear from our study of Paul's admonitions to the believer about family relationships. For example, we cannot take Paul's teachings and use them to justify the continuation of slavery. We believe that the abolition of slavery was right and that it was demanded by the Christian gospel.

Also, a vast change has occurred in the immediate family. In the first century, most women were dependent totally on men for their support. But in more and more American families, the responsibility for earning a living is shared by husbands and wives. This partnership in earning a living certainly calls for some basic changes in the structure of the family. For example, if the wife is employed the task of housework should be shared by the husband. Many other implications for the family structure arise from the modern situation.

But one thing is unchanging. If a person is a Christian, his or her relationships to other family members are brought under the lordship of Christ. Forms change, but that which is vital and which makes life meaningful does not change. That we adhere to some procedure or form that cannot be made to fit the demands of life as it is is not important. But that we love one another is important. That each Christian member of the group have a great concern for the welfare, growth, and happiness of the others is imperative.

Today is the age of narcissism—an inordinate emphasis on and concern for ourselves. Narcissism is self-defeating in the long run. The person who is concerned only for self ultimately will be cut off from other people. The true self is discovered and experienced only in relationship to others. This is true especially with reference to the family.

Personal Learning Activities

1. When Paul charged wives to be subject to their husbands, he argued for innate male superiority. True____ False____

2. According to Paul, the husband's attitude toward the wife is to be one of (choose the proper response):

_____(1) Arrogance

_____(2) Love

_____(3) Tolerance

_   (4) Sternness

3. In Paul's view, the destiny of the church was to (select the proper answer):

_____(1) Become large

_____(2) Become wealthy

_____(3) Be made to have the character of a perfect offering

_____(4) Become ineffective and cease to exist

4. Paul had in mind a Christian family when he admonished children to obey their parents. True_____ False_____

5. Paul did not advocate the abolition of slavery because (select the proper responses):

_____(1) Christians constituted a small minority.

_____(2) The economic system was not built on free labor.

_____(3) Paul was not a social reformer in the modern sense.

6. The kind of freedom Paul visualized for believers was freedom in the area of _____. (Choose the proper answer.)

(1) Finances

(2) Opportunity

(3) Attitude

(4) Social acceptance

7. How do you apply Paul's words about the service of slaves and the attitude of masters to today's world?

10

Preparation for the Battle

Ephesians 6:10-24

We have come to the closing section of Ephesians. Paul had described for the readers how the mighty purpose of God's love had culminated in the creation of the church. He had set before them the direction in which God is moving his people. He had taught them what it meant to be God's people in an evil world. He was ready to take leave of them.

As Paul prepared to close his letter, however, his major concern was with the present Christian struggle. He was acutely aware of the great power arrayed against God's new people. He knew how easily an unprepared believer succumbs to the force of evil.

Paul used his closing remarks, therefore, in the attempt to help the struggling believers take a firm stance in life. Hostile powers engaged them in an effort to destroy God's work. The apostle wanted to equip his readers for ultimate victory over threatening forces.

The Nature of the Battle (6:10-13)

Above all else, the readers needed strength for the struggle in which they were engaged. Consequently, Paul enjoined them to "be strong" (v. 10). This verb may be understood better as passive and translated, be strengthened.

Whatever the translation, Paul did not mean for Christians to rely on their own inner resources. The strength they needed came from outside themselves. They were strong only when they were strengthened by their God. This concept of receiving strength is made clear by the addition of the phrase "in the Lord and in the strength of his might" (v. 10). This phrase reminds us of the request Paul made on behalf of his readers in Ephesians 1:19. There, Paul asked that they might know the greatness of God's power. This is the power that had raised Jesus from the dead and had elevated him to his position of sovereign authority. It was also the power operative in the redemption of believers.

Paul had no doubt that this power was available to people for their continuing struggles in the world. God's power already had manifested its invincible character. Believers needed to be aware of it and be confident that it was available to them "in the Lord" (v. 10)—by virtue of their relationship to the risen and conquering Savior.

In order to drive home the resources that were available to his readers, Paul used a military metaphor. He was familiar with the equipment of the Roman soldier from his encounters with the Roman legions in his travels. As he wrote these verses, one or more guards might have been at his side to guard him in his imprisonment.

Believers also were engaged in a warfare for which they desperately needed the proper equipment, and Paul had total confidence that the equipment was available. All Christians had to do was to use it. Therefore, Paul urged the believers to "put on the whole armor of God" (v. 11). Some question exists about whether "whole armor" is the correct translation of the underlying Greek word. From the pieces of equipment cited below, Paul clearly had the picture of the armed foot soldier in mind. But, even so, some important pieces of equipment are missing from the list.

Paul described the Christian soldier's equipment as the "armor of God." This phrase is ambiguous in both Greek and English. It may mean God's own armor. From his Old Testament background, Paul was familiar with the notion that God was a warrior and with the idea that he used pieces of armor in his battle against his enemies. So, the idea may be that God shares his own armor with those who battle with him.

Whether this be true or not, "the whole armor of God" is what God provides for the Christian. The believer is not defenseless in the face of evil's assault. The Christian may receive the armor that God provides, and that individual may put it on.

The necessity for the armor is highlighted in the last part of verse 11: "That you may be able to stand against the wiles of the devil." The verb "stand" is used in a metaphorical and military sense. When the soldier falls in the field of battle, he is defeated. The soldier's ultimate purpose is to be standing at the end of the battle while his foe lies vanquished at his

Roman armor

feet.

The situation and challenge confronting the Christian soldier are rendered doubly serious by the identity of the enemy and the nature of his attack. The enemy is the "devil." Paul generally did not use personal names like this for the believers' antagonist. He usually employed terms like sin, flesh, this age.

The devil's attack is not open, direct, and honest. It is deceitful. The enemy will use every stratagem in order to achieve his desired goal—the downfall of the believer.

Paul went on to elucidate his point by adding a negative remark: "We are not contending against flesh and blood" (v. 12). The *Today's English Version* translates the idea correctly: "We are not fighting against human beings."

For us to bear in mind that we are not fighting against flesh and blood is essential. The Christian community often confuses the issue by making people the object of attack. We are not fighting against people. We are in a warfare against those forces that victimize and destroy people.

Our enemy is not another person. If we fail in Christian living, we will not do so because of the attack of an individual or a group. We will fail because our own spirit's inner fortress has been breached by the power of evil.

Indeed, in our expressions of hostility and our desire for vengeance on others, evil is able to overcome us. Paul saw this and wrote about it in Romans 12:19-21.

Paul believed that the church was involved in a warfare of cosmic dimensions. The battle was "against the principalities, against the powers, against the world rulers of this present darkness" (v. 12). We have encountered this terminology before in Ephesians (1:21). We also find it elsewhere in Paul's writings (Rom. 8:38-39; Col. 1:16). Such terminology was in vogue in the religious thought of the time.

Paul saw the danger confronting Christians in the most serious light. Nevertheless, he was confident that the power of God was greater than the spiritual powers. In Jesus Christ, God had gained the decisive victory over the threatening powers; the Christians had been delivered from the spiritual powers' dominion. Furthermore, Christians have the resources to resist any power that assaults them with the confidence of overcoming it.

"The spiritual hosts of wickedness in the heavenly places" (v. 12) is a general description of the forces available to the threatening powers. The word "hosts" is not in the Greek text. However, this word or some other must be supplied to give meaning to the statement. Other translations have readings like "superhuman forces" (NEB) and "spiritual army."[1] This army is engaged in a spiritual conflict, a contrast to the world's armies that are interested in capturing towns and countries and in acquisition of earthly treasures.

The spiritual forces are found "in heavenly places" (v. 12). That is, their power transcends any earthly power. They contend with God not only on the earth, but also in the domain that we think of as belonging to him. Perhaps this idea is parallel to "the power of the air" (Eph. 2:2) that we have discussed already.

Paul was certain that the "evil day" (v. 13) would come for his readers. This evil day would be the day of vicious assault and supreme testing by the spiritual forces arrayed against the church. Therefore, Christians would need to put on God's armor at once in order to be ready for their trial by fire.

The Christian's Armor (6:14-17)

The first item of military equipment to be donned by the Christian soldier is the girdle of truth (v. 14). The reference is an obvious echo of Isaiah 11:5 where righteousness is the girdle around the waist of the Davidic Messiah. In Ephesians, this figure is transferred to the believer.

We have suggested that the armor of the contemporary Roman foot soldier furnished Paul the images for his metaphors. In this case, the girdle was a kind of leather apron worn under the armor to protect the thighs.

"Truth" is not to be understood in any subjective way. To Paul, truth was above all the divine reality which had come to believers through Jesus Christ. This reality will help them ward off the devil's deceptive attacks. The devil will try to convince God's people that falsehood is truth; that the way of destruction is the way of life; that one gains life by saving it; that what is important is money, power, sexual gratification. But, armed with God's truth, believers will be in touch with reality and will be able to resist all such attacks.

The second piece of equipment is the "breastplate of righteousness" (v. 14). This figure goes back to the statement found in Isaiah 59:17. In the Old Testament passage, righteousness is a part of God's own armor that he puts on as he prepares to intervene on behalf of his people. In that context, it is God's own righteousness—his justice and his opposition to evil—that is in view.

Some question exists about how we are to understand righteousness in the Ephesians passage. Generally, Paul emphasized that God gives righteousness to the person who believes in Jesus Christ. This prevailing concept does not rule out a second possibility. Paul may have had in mind the righteousness or uprightness of the believer. Indeed, the two cannot be separated, as we have seen in Ephesians.

So, the breastplate of righteousness may be the believer's new stand before God as a justified sinner. But it probably includes the faithful commitment of the believer to the holy God who saved him. The devil's attempts to tempt the Christian will be frustrated by this breastplate of righteousness.

Once again, Paul referred to a passage in Isaiah in his description of the third piece of Christian armor. In Isaiah 52:7, the prophet extolled the beauty of God's feet as God approached to bring the good news of peace.

In Ephesians, "the gospel of peace" (v. 15) is the good news of salvation through Jesus Christ. The good news declares that peace exists between God and his child and also can become a reality among all his children.

The shoes which furnish the background of the metaphor were those worn by the Roman legionnaries. Their shoes were half boots with a strong sole and open leather work above.

Numerous interpretations are given to the word translated "equipment" in the Revised Standard Version and "preparation" in the King James Version. One possibility is the translation given by *The Jerusalem Bible.* There, the shoes are "the eagerness to spread the gospel of peace."[2] A telling argument is posed against this translation. All the other pieces of equipment are defensive in nature. Indeed, this listing of defensive pieces is in keeping with the purpose of the armor as announced by Paul in verse 11. According to *The New English Bible,* for example, the shoes are themselves "the gospel of peace"; the purpose of the shoes is "to give you firm footing" (v. 15, NEB). If this is the correct idea, the text teaches that the believer is to keep his or her feet firmly planted in the gospel. This will assure the Christian of being able to stand against the devil's assaults. The purpose of those assaults is to make one doubt the truth of the gospel, to cut off the believer from a close, vital relationship with God, and to cause one to accept a false source of security.

In addition to the three previously mentioned items, Paul urged his readers to take up "the shield of faith" (v. 16). The shield which furnished the metaphor was large and oblong. Polybius gave the dimensions as 4 by 2½ feet. Thus, the shield was able to defend effectively the whole body.

In warfare, arrows could be dipped in pitch and set afire before being shot at the enemy. The foot soldier's defense against these flaming arrows was his large body shield that fended them off and caused them to fall harmlessly to the ground.

In the Christian's armor, faith is the shield. Faith is not to be understood in terms of adherence to a prescribed body of doctrine. Rather, it is a personal commitment to Jesus Christ and a personal relationship with him marked by confidence and trust.

The devil will attempt to separate the believer from Christ as he assaults the believer with doubts. But personal faith which is the result of a personal relationship with the Lord will enable the believer to extinguish all of the devil's flaming arrows of doubt, suspicion, and fear.

The helmet that God provides is "salvation" (v. 17). But in Isaiah 59:17, God puts on "a helmet of salvation" as he prepares for his decisive intervention in the affairs of people. In that context, God will provide salvation for his people as he exercises his righteous judgment. In Jewish literature, God is presented as adorning the Messiah with the helmet of salvation.

Paul used the "helmet of salvation" with a different application—the believer puts on the "helmet of salvation" which God provides. The Christian is secure in the confidence that God is his/her ultimate hope. Nothing can separate the believer from the love of God. Ultimate victory and vindication are assured.

The Christian soldier is armed with only one offensive weapon. Yet, its use probably was defensive in the context of Ephesians 6:14-17. The one offensive weapon is the "sword of the Spirit" (v. 17). The Spirit is not the sword, rather the Spirit provides it. The sword is identified as the "word of God" (v. 17). From the Spirit, the believer receives God's appropriate word in his or her life situations.

The word of God could refer to the gospel message. We probably are closer to the meaning, however, when we think of the way Jesus used the word of God in his trials in the desert region. In each case, he fended off the devil's temptations with the word of God. Or, we can remember Jesus' assurance to his followers: At times when they would be beleaguered by their persecutors, the Spirit would give them the word from God to respond to their accusers (Matt. 10:19). This idea fits exactly the context of the passage from Ephesians.

In the believers' conflict with the forces of evil in the world, they are not to use the world's weapons. How tragic that people who claimed to be Jesus' followers have so marred Christian history by deeds of violence and bloodshed! His followers have only one weapon—the word of God—which the Spirit gives to them.

The Call to Prayer (6:18-20)

The absolute necessity for prayer in the Christian life is the subject of 6:18-20. One question that is raised concerns the relationship of prayer to the armor. Is prayer the seventh piece of the Christian armor? This is a possibility.

More likely, Paul's comments on prayer were an explanation of his metaphor about the believer's military equipment. How do Christians arm themselves? The answer is: through prayer. Through prayer, the believing community expresses its complete dependence on God. From God, the community receives what it needs to stand firm before the onslaught of evil and hostile powers.

As may be seen from the translation of verse 18, the word "all" occurs four times. This repetition emphasizes that the life of the believer is a life of prayer. This is another way of saying that the Christian is dependent completely on God.

The Christian is to "pray at all times" (v. 18) or at every opportunity. Paul added "in the Spirit." This distinguishes Christian prayer from pagan prayer. The Spirit's presence in our lives inspires us to pray, enables us to pray, and determines the character of our prayers. *The New English Bible* interprets the phrase to mean "in the power of the Spirit." The *Today's English Version* translates: "as the Spirit leads." Both translations give an aspect of what praying "in the Spirit" means, but the meaning of the phrase is larger than either rendering.

The believer is to pray "with all prayer and supplication" (v. 18). This phrase probably means that every form of prayer should be used. The word for prayer used here is a general term that denotes calling on God. "Supplication" or petition is one form of prayer. The word may be used with reference either to God or man. Paul probably mentioned this form because supplication is the Christian community's responsibility and privilege that he emphasized in the passage. Christian prayer also includes forms like praise and thanksgiving.

The mental and spiritual attitude appropriate to prayer is alertness. The community is not to become spiritually drowsy; it is not to fall asleep. It is to be like an army, always on the alert, aware that crises and challenges may arise at any moment. The Christian community never takes anything for granted, but recognizes that, at every moment, its existence depends on God.

"Keep alert" is modified by the phrase "with all perseverance" (v. 18). The community's commitment to prayer is total; no interruption, no flagging may be allowed in its adherence to prayer.

Finally, prayer is not self-centered. It looks outward. The believer is to pray tenaciously "for all the staints" (v. 18). Here, Paul underlined the interdependence of the Christian community. The life of faith is not a solitary life. Every Christian requires the support of his brothers and sisters constantly. Paul's ideal for the church is seen in this united fellowship where love for others is expressed in constant, serious, intercessory prayer.

Paul included himself in the company of saints for whom believers were to pray. The meaning of "and also for me" (v. 19) can be: and especially for me. Paul felt a special need for the prayers of other Christians. But Paul did not want his welfare, safety, or release from prison to be his brothers' and sisters' special concern when they prayed for him. He was interested primarily in the gospel and in his role in its proclamation. The physical circumstances of his life were always of secondary importance to him.

Paul asked that his readers pray for two things. (1) When God opened

Paul's mouth, Paul wanted to be sure that he would have something to say. He wanted to speak God's message at the appropriate moment (v. 19).

(2) Paul wanted to have boldness or, perhaps better, freedom, when he proclaimed the gospel (v. 19). The "gospel" is the "mystery." The gospel is the revelation from God that had been given to people through Jesus Christ. It revealed that God's purpose in Christ was to create his new people from Jews and Gentiles. Paul wanted to preach this gospel in all its fullness, without any inner restraint.

Paul considered himself to be Christ's ambassador or envoy in the world (2 Cor. 5:20). Here, he called himself an ambassador for the gospel (v. 20). This simply described the purpose of his mission. He represented Christ in the world on behalf of the gospel.

For those of us who read this letter, irony is present in the words "in chains" (v. 20). While Rome entertained and honored ambassadors from earthly kings, the greatest of all ambassadors was one of her prisoners. If people only had known that this apparently powerless, unpretentious little Jew was the representative to them from God's royal court!

But the chains did not change Paul's divine assignment. Instead they were the sign of it, for he was in a realm hostile to his King. Paul did not become bitter at the outward circumstances of his life. He did not ask that they be changed. He was in touch with God's eternal reality and was not perturbed by the temporary, passing manifestations of the power of evil.

The Conclusion (6:21-24)

Paul's pastoral concern permeates the epistle's closing statements. Much remained about him personally that Paul had not told his readers. They would be anxious for more information. Those details would be supplied by Tychicus when he arrived with Paul's letter.

Acts 20:4 reveals that Tychicus was a native of the province of Asia; he was with Paul in Greece. He was one of the churches' representatives commissioned to take an offering to the believers in Jerusalem at the end of Paul's third missionary journey. He also is mentioned in Colossians 4:7; 2 Timothy 4:12; and Titus 3:12.

Paul's attitude toward Tychicus was expressed in Paul's description of him. He was a "beloved brother and faithful minister" (v. 21). "Faithful minister" probably should be understood as "trustworthy helper" (NEB). The word for minister is *diakonos,* which may be translated in various ways in the New Testament. Helper is a good translation here. This translation also points the way to the understanding of the function of the deacon (also *diakonos*) in the early church.

Not only would Tychicus be able to give factual information about Paul, but he also would be able to perform a ministry among the readers. He would "encourage [their] hearts" (v. 22). Perhaps Paul thought that news about his sufferings might drain other Christians of their nerve and joy in Christian living. Tychicus could help them see that Paul's imprisonment was a victory rather than a failure of the gospel.

The closing blessing is unusual in Paul's writings. Peace, or grace, or grace and love normally are found in other letters. Here peace, love, grace, and faith are linked together (vv. 23-24). We already have looked at these words in other contexts in Ephesians.

One other unusual characteristic may be mentioned. "Grace" is placed last, whereas it comes first elsewhere in Paul's letters. Logically, it belongs in first place. Grace is that undeserved love of God which is the reason for, and the source of, all that he does. Our new standing with him (peace) and our new relationship with one another (also peace) are due solely to grace. As believers, Paul's readers already had experienced peace, love, and faith because of God's grace. But Paul believed that what they had known was but an indication of the Christian life's possibilities. God still could give more and more.

God's blessings rest on those who have responded to his redemptive activity and "who love our Lord Jesus Christ" (v. 24). Some question exists about the exact meaning and relationship of the last phrase in the letter which the Revised Standard Version translates with the word "undying." Literally, it may be translated: in incorruption or in immortality. The Revised Standard Version's translators chose the former and linked it with love. *The Jerusalem Bible* and *The New English Bible's* translators chose the latter and linked the phrase with grace. *The Jerusalem Bible* has "may grace and eternal life be with all who love our Lord Jesus Christ."[3] Both are possibilities, and both are true. Those who belong to God love Jesus Christ with an incorruptible or undying love. Those who by God's grace participate in the new community that he creates can have the confidence that their new life is eternal.

"Thanks be to God for his inexpressible gift" (2 Cor. 9:15).

The Seriousness of the Conflict Today

To live the Christian life is not easy. This is one major truth emerging from a study of Paul's writings. He viewed the matter of living by the truth of Christ with utmost seriousness.

We cannot help noticing the difference between Paul's view of Christian living and the contemporary view of many church members. Apparently, for many of us, sin and evil are not serious realities. Many people seem to take a rather flippant attitude toward Christian morality; failure in this area is not thought to be serious.

One reason for our casual attitude is the differing circumstances under which we live. To become a believer in those early days was an extremely serious matter. Oftentimes, to become a Christian meant that one would be persecuted, cut off from family, and ostracized by society. The challenge to the believer's commitment was real, constant, and obvious.

In our culture, to be identified with the church usually does not cost anything. People generally do not lose their jobs, their families, or their friends. In many of our communities, no great contrast is evident between the Christian and the non-Christian world. Many of us do not have a sense of being assaulted or embattled by forces that are seeking to exterminate the gospel.

When we understand the Christian life properly, however, living the Christian way is still difficult. To maintain integrity as a business person in a society where deception has become so widespread and accepted is difficult. To deal with the problems of prejudice, to be open to all God's people of whatever race or class, is no easier now than it was in the first century. To trust in God absolutely for our security and not in money or position is still difficult.

We continue to need all the help God is ready to give his children in order for our lives to be constant witnesses to our relationship with Christ. We still need the whole armor of God.

---

1. *The Jerusalem Bible* (Garden City, New York: Doubleday & Co., Inc. 1966), p. 336.

2. *Ibid.*, p. 336.

3. *Ibid.*, p. 337.

Personal Learning Activities

1. What Paul's readers needed above all else for their struggle against threatening forces was _____. Choose the correct response.
   (1) Strength
   (2) Money
   (3) Political power
   (4) Organization

2. If we fail in Christian living, we will not do so because of attack by an individual or a group; we will fail because the inner fortress of our own spirit has been breached by the power of evil. True _____ False _____

3. Paul employed the metaphor of armor to emphasize what God provides for the Christian in the continuing struggle with evil. Match the two lists, linking the piece of armor with its spiritual equivalent:

_____(1) Girdle	(a) Righteousness
_____(2) Breastplate	(b) Salvation
_____(3) Shoes	(c) Truth
_____(4) Shield	(d) Word of God
_____(5) Helmet	(e) Faith
_____(6) Sword	(f) Gospel

4. According to Paul, the Christian community is to pray (select the proper responses from the list):

_____(1) At all times

_____(2) In the spirit

_____(3) Without lagging

_____(4) With every form of prayers

_____(5) In alertness

_____(6) For all the saints

5. Paul closed Ephesians with a blessing in which he included four great words from his vocabulary. From the list, select the four gifts he wanted for his readers:

_____(1) Grace

_____(2) Wisdom

_____(3) Peace

_____(4) Ability

_____(5) Love

_____(6) Faith

Answers:
1. (1); 2. *True;* 3. (1)c, (2)a, (3)f, (4)e, (5)b, (6)d;   4. (1), (2), (3), (4), (5), (6); 5. (1), (3), (5), (6).

THE CHURCH STUDY COURSE

The Church Study Course consists of a variety of short-term credit courses for adults and youth and noncredit foundational units for children and preschoolers. The materials are for use in addition to the study and training curriculums made available to the churches on an ongoing basis.

Study courses and foundational units are organized into a system that is promoted by the Sunday School Board, 127 Ninth Avenue, North, Nashville, Tennessee 37234, by the Woman's Missionary Union, 600 North Twentieth Street, Birmingham, Alabama 35203; by the Brotherhood Commission, 1548 Poplar Avenue, Memphis, Tennessee 38104; and by the respective departments of the state conventions affiliated with the Southern Baptist Convention.

Study course materials are flexible enough to be adapted to the needs of any Baptist church. The resources are published in several different formats—textbooks of various sizes, workbooks, and kits. Each item contains a brief explanation of the Church Study Course and information on requesting credit. Additional information and interpretation are available from the participating agencies.

Types of Study and Credit

Adults and youth can earn study course credit through individual or group study. Teachers of courses or of foundational units also are eligible to receive credit.

1. Class Experience.—Group involvement with course material for the designated number of hours for the particular course.
   A person who is absent from one or more sessions must complete the "Personal Learning Activities" or other requirements for the course.
2. Individual Study.—This includes reading, viewing, or listening to course material and completing the specified requirements for the course.
3. Lesson Course Study.—Parallel use of designated study course material during the study of selected units in Church Program Organization periodical curriculum units. Guidance for this means of credit appears in the selected periodical.
4. Institutional Study.—Parallel use of designated study course material during regular courses at educational institutions, including Seminary Extension Department courses. Guidance for this means of credit is provided by the teacher.

Credit is awarded for the successful completion of a course of study. This credit is granted by the Church Study Course Awards Office, 127 Ninth Avenue, North, Nashville, Tennessee 37234, for the participating agencies. Form 151 (available free) is recommended for use in requesting credit.

When credit is issued to a person on request, the Awards Office sends two copies of a notice of credit earned to the church. The original copy of the credit slip should be filed by the study course clerk in the participant's record of training folder. The duplicate should be given to the person who earned the credit. Accumulated credits are applied toward leadership or member development diplomas, which are measures of learning, growth, development, and training.

Detailed information about the Church Study Course system of credits, diplomas, and record keeping is available from the participating agencies. Study course materials, supplementary teaching or learning aids, and forms for record keeping may be ordered from Baptist Book Stores.

The Church Study Course Curriculum
Credit is granted on those courses listed in the current copy of *Church Services and Materials Catalog* and *Baptist Book Store Catalog*. When selecting courses or foundational units, check the current catalogs to determine what study course materials are valid.

How to Request Credit for This Course
This book is the text for a course in the subject area Bible Studies.

This course is designed for 6 hours of group study. Credit is awarded for satisfactory class experience with the study material for the minimum number of hours. A person who is absent from one or more sessions must complete the "Personal Learning Activities" or other requirements for the materials missed.

Credit is also allowed for use of this material in individual study and in institutional study, if so designated.

The following requirements must be met for credit in this course:
1. Read the book *Ephesians: God's New People*.
2. Attend at least 6 hours of class study or complete all "Personal Learning Activities" (see end of each chapter). A class member who is absent from one or more class sessions must complete "Personal Learning Activities" on chapters missed. In such a case, he or she must turn in his/her paper by the date the teacher sets, usually within ten days following the last class.

Credit in this course may be earned through individual study. The requirements for such credit are:
1. Read the book.

2. Complete the "Personal Learning Activities" on the chapters.

Credit in this course may be earned through study in an educational institution, if so designated by a teacher. The requirements are:

1. Read the book.

2. Fulfill the requirements of the course taught at the institution.

After the course is completed, the teacher, the study course records librarian, the learner, or any person designated by the church should complete Form 151 ("Church Study Course Credit Request, Revised 1975") and send it to the Awards Office, 127 Ninth Avenue, North, Nashville, Tennessee 37234. In the back of this book the reader will find a form which he may cut out, fill in, and send to the Awards Office.

INSTRUCTIONS: If requested by the teacher, fill in this form and give it to him when the course is completed. If preferred, mail this request for course credit to

AWARDS OFFICE
THE SUNDAY SCHOOL BOARD, SBC
127 NINTH AVENUE, NORTH
NASHVILLE, TENNESSEE 37234

CHURCH		
State Convention	Association	
Church Name		
Mailing Address		
City, State, Zip Code		

Indicate Type of Study (X)

☐ Class ☐ Individual ☐ Lesson Course ☐ Educational Institution

MAIL TO

Mail to (If Different from Church Address)

Street, Route, or P.O. Box

City, State, Zip Code

LAST NAME	FIRST NAME AND MIDDLE INITIAL	MRS. (X)	COURSE TITLE
			Ephesians: God's New People